rose
une rose
eine Rose

pussy willow
les chatons de saule
die Weidenkätzchen

cat
le chat
die Katze

football
le ballon
der Fußball

Indian
un Indien
ein Indianer

toad
le crapaud
die Kröte

raccoon
le raton laveur
der Waschbär

drum
le tambour
die Trommel

toadstool
le champignon vénéneux
der Giftpilz

horse
le cheval
das Pferd

dragonfly
une libellule
eine Libelle

rabbit
le lapin
der Hase

nurse
une infirmière
die Krankenschwester

patient
le malade
der Patient

bugle
le clairon
das Waldhorn

fox
le renard
der Fuchs

beaver
le castor
der Biber

witch
une sorcière
eine Hexe

broom
le balai
der Besen

black cat
un chat noir
eine schwarze Katze

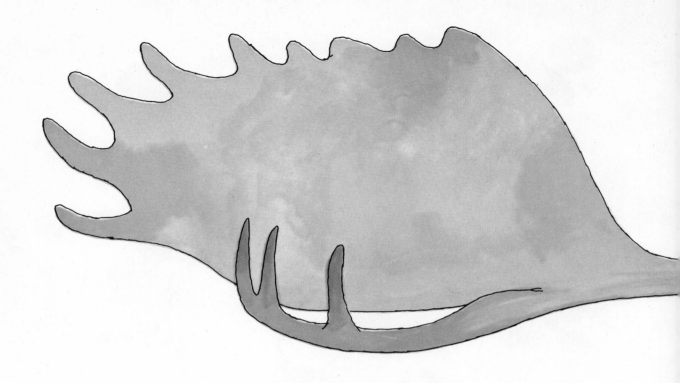

Dear Children,

Perhaps you know that in both French and German words are pronounced very differently. If you are already learning a foreign language at school, ask your teacher how to say the words in this book the correct way. If not, ask any grown-up who speaks the language – or, best of all, a friend from France or Germany.

Happy Holidays!

Richard Scarry

mosquito
le moustique
der Moskito

HAMLYN
London · New York · Sydney · Toronto

moth
une mite
eine Motte

RICHARD SCARRY'S

EUROPEAN WORD BOOK

ENGLISH · FRENCH · GERMAN

mouse
une souris
eine Maus

moss
la mousse
das Moos

moose
un élan
der Elch

mushroom
le champignon
der Pilz

bear
un ours
der Bär

paper aeroplane
un avion en papier
das Papierflugzeug

CONTENTS

hoop
le cerceau
der Reifen

cat
le chat
die Katze

This edition first published 1974 by
The Hamlyn Publishing Group Limited
London · New York · Sydney · Toronto
Astronaut House, Feltham, Middlesex, England
by arrangement with Western Publishing Company Inc.
Ninth impression 1983

Printed and bound in Spain
by Graficromo, S. A. – Córdoba
ISBN 0 600 38144 7
The illustrations in this book first appeared in
Richard Scarry's BEST WORD BOOK EVER,
first published in 1964.

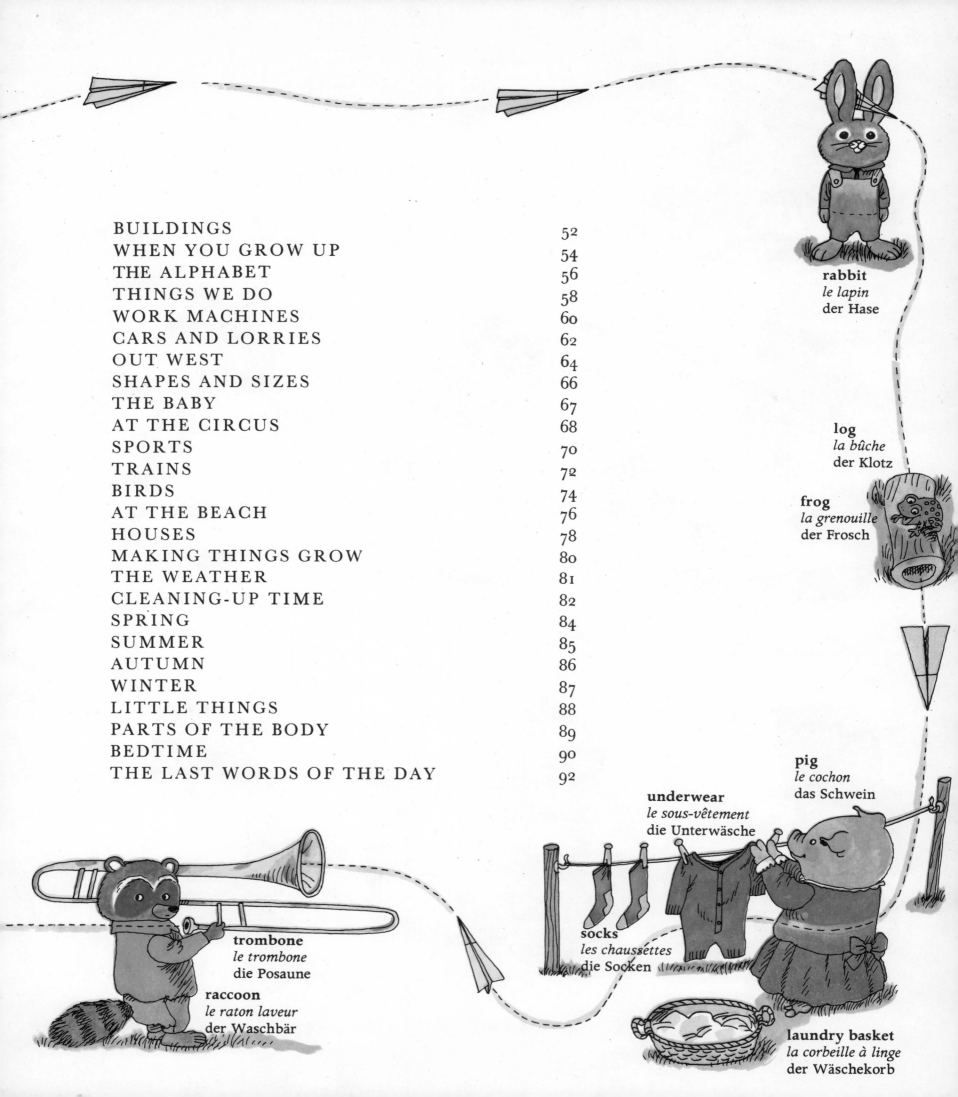

rabbit
le lapin
der Hase

log
la bûche
der Klotz

frog
la grenouille
der Frosch

pig
le cochon
das Schwein

underwear
le sous-vêtement
die Unterwäsche

trombone
le trombone
die Posaune

raccoon
le raton laveur
der Waschbär

socks
les chaussettes
die Socken

laundry basket
la corbeille à linge
der Wäschekorb

curtains
les rideaux
die Vorhänge

sun
le soleil
die Sonne

window
la fenêtre
das Fenster

THE NEW DAY

It is the morning of a new day.
The sun is shining.
Little Bear gets up out of bed.

Little Bear gets up
Petit Ours se lève
Der kleine Bär steht auf

face cloth
le gant de toilette
der Waschlappen

soap
le savon
die Seife

towel
la serviette
das Handtuch

First he washes his face and hands,
D'abord il se lave la figure et les mains,
Zuerst wäscht er sich Gesicht und Hände,

toothbrush
la brosse à dents
die Zahnbürste

toothpaste
le dentifrice
die Zahnpaste

then he brushes his teeth
puis il se brosse les dents.
dann putzt er sich die Zähne

mirror
la glace
der Spiegel

comb
le peigne
der Kamm

pyjamas
le pyjama
das Pyjama

and combs his hair.
et se peigne.
und kämmt sich seine Haare.

shirt
la chemise
das Hemd

trousers
le pantalon
die Hose

He dresses himself.
Il s'habille.
Er zieht sich an.

He makes his bed.
Il fait son lit.
Er macht sein Bett.

He comes promptly when he is called to breakfast.
Il accourt, dès qu'on l'appelle pour le petit déjeuner.
Er kommt sofort, wenn er zum Frühstück gerufen wird.

8

The bear sits straight up in his chair.
L'ours se tient droit sur sa chaise.
Der Bär sitzt ganz gerade auf seinem Stuhl.

He is very hungry. This is what he eats:
Il a grand-faim. Voici ce qu'il mange:
Er ist sehr hungrig. Dies alles ißt er:

fruit juice
un jus de fruit
Obstsaft

porridge with cream
du porridge avec de la crème fraîche
Haferbrei mit Rahm

pancakes
des crêpes
Pfannkuchen

with butter and syrup
avec du beurre et de la mélasse
mit Butter und Sirup

He does not eat
the toaster.
*Il ne mange pas
le grille-pain.*
Den Toaströster
ißt er nicht.

fried eggs
des oeufs sur le plat
Spiegeleier

bacon
du bacon
Speck

toast
des toasts
Toast

muffins
des muffins (petit pain anglais)
Muffins (englisches Teegebäck)

honey
du miel
Honig

jam
de la confiture
Marmelade

cocoa
du cacao
Kakao

cold milk and a waffle
du lait froid et une gaufre
kalte Milch und eine Waffel

When he has finished eating breakfast he helps his mother to wash up.
Quand il a terminé son petit déjeuner, il aide sa mère à faire la vaisselle.
Wenn er mit dem Frühstück fertig ist, hilft er seiner Mutter beim Abspülen.

cup
une tasse
eine Tasse

saucer
une soucoupe
eine Untertasse

plate
une assiette
der Teller

bowl
le bol
die Schüssel

fork
la fourchette
die Gabel

knife
le couteau
das Messer

spoon
la cuiller
der Löffel

glass
le verre
das Glas

lid
le couvercle
der Deckel

jam jar
le pot de confiture
das Einmachglas

jug
le pot
der Krug

frying pan
la poêle
die Bratpfanne

pot
la casserole
der Topf

pan
le plat
der Tiegel

bottle
la bouteille
die Flasche

lemon squeezer
le presse-citron
die Saftpresse

glass
le verre
das Glas

Now he is ready to play with his friends.
Maintenant, il peut jouer avec ses amis.
Jetzt kann er mit seinen Freunden spielen.

THE RABBIT FAMILY'S HOUSE

Father Rabbit, Mother Rabbit, and the
Rabbit Brothers are getting ready for
the new day. Their friend Owl
is waiting for the two brothers
to come out to play.
Can you find him?

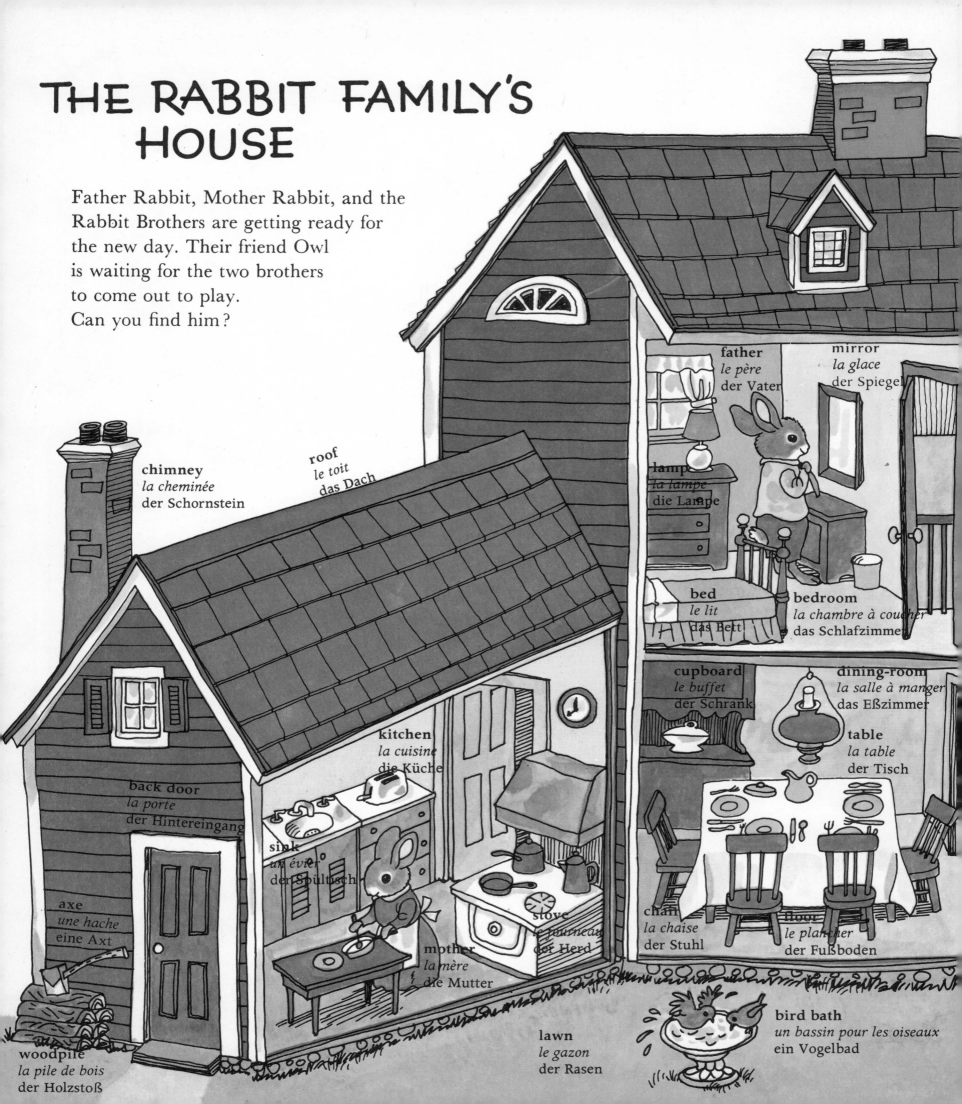

chimney
la cheminée
der Schornstein

roof
le toit
das Dach

father
le père
der Vater

mirror
la glace
der Spiegel

lamp
la lampe
die Lampe

bed
le lit
das Bett

bedroom
la chambre à coucher
das Schlafzimmer

cupboard
le buffet
der Schrank

dining-room
la salle à manger
das Eßzimmer

table
la table
der Tisch

kitchen
la cuisine
die Küche

back door
la porte
der Hintereingang

sink
un évier
der Spültisch

axe
une hache
eine Axt

stove
le fourneau
der Herd

chair
la chaise
der Stuhl

floor
le plancher
der Fußboden

mother
la mère
die Mutter

woodpile
la pile de bois
der Holzstoß

lawn
le gazon
der Rasen

bird bath
un bassin pour les oiseaux
ein Vogelbad

owl
le hibou
die Eule

television aerial
une antenne de télévision
eine Fernsehantenne

smoke
la fumée
der Rauch

light switch
un interrupteur
der Lichtschalter

armchair
le fauteuil
der Sessel

television set
le poste de télévision
der Fernsehapparat

record player
un électrophone
der Plattenspieler

beds
les couchettes
die Betten

bathroom
la salle de bains
das Badezimmer

staircase
le palier
das Treppenhaus

front door
la porte d'entrée
die Haustür

boy's bedroom
la chambre des garçons
das Bubenschlafzimmer

living-room
le salon
das Wohnzimmer

candle
la chandelle
die Kerze

telephone
le téléphone
das Telefon

fireplace
la cheminée
der Kamin

window
la fenêtre
das Fenster

picture
le tableau
das Bild

stairs
l'escalier
die Treppe

sofa
le canapé
das Sofa

front hall
le vestibule
die Diele

doormat
le paillasson
die Fußmatte

stone path
le dallage
der Plattenweg

rug
le tapis
der Teppich

11

AT THE PLAYGROUND

The children are all having fun doing
different things. Which children are
doing the things you like best?

see-saw
le tapecul
die Wippe

slide
le toboggan
die Rutschbahn

leapfrog
jouer à saute-mouton
das Bockspringen

somersault
la cabriole
der Purzelbaum

hide-and-seek
jouer à cache-cache
das Versteckspiel

ring-a-ring-o'-roses
la ronde
der Ringelreihen

skipping a rope
sauter à la corde
das Seilspringen

ladder
une échelle
eine Leiter

rings
les anneaux
die Ringe

swing
une balançoire
eine Schaukel

sliding pole
le mât
die Kletterstange

top
la toupie
der Kreisel

roller skates
les patins à roulettes
die Rollschuhe

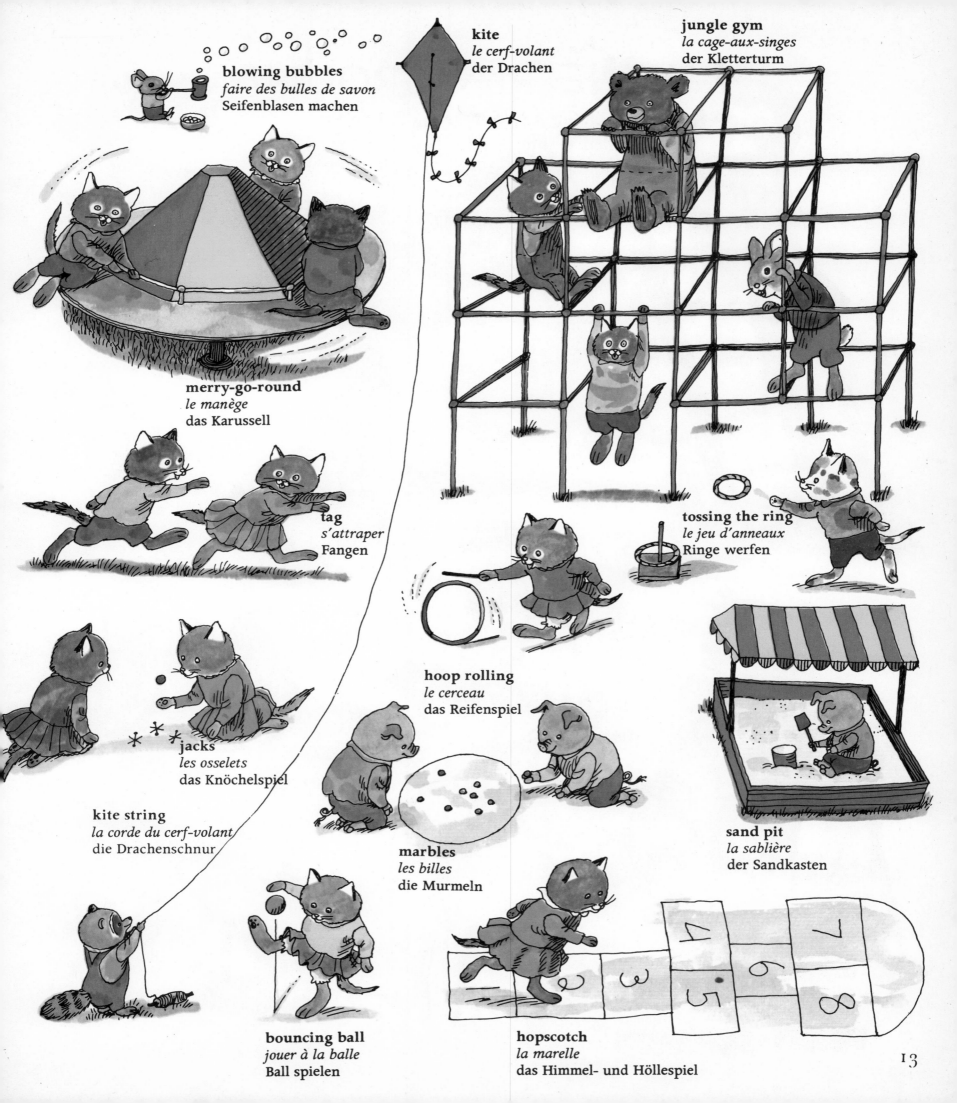

blowing bubbles
faire des bulles de savon
Seifenblasen machen

kite
le cerf-volant
der Drachen

jungle gym
la cage-aux-singes
der Kletterturm

merry-go-round
le manège
das Karussell

tag
s'attraper
Fangen

tossing the ring
le jeu d'anneaux
Ringe werfen

jacks
les osselets
das Knöchelspiel

hoop rolling
le cerceau
das Reifenspiel

kite string
la corde du cerf-volant
die Drachenschnur

marbles
les billes
die Murmeln

sand pit
la sablière
der Sandkasten

bouncing ball
jouer à la balle
Ball spielen

hopscotch
la marelle
das Himmel- und Höllespiel

13

TOOLS

hammer
le marteau
der Hammer

nail
le clou
der Nagel

Everyone is very busy
working with his tools.
Who always carries his
tool with him?
He has a red head.

drawing pin
la punaise
die Reißzwecke

axe
la hache
die Axt

ladder
une échelle
eine Leiter

carpenter
le menuisier
der Tischler

board
la planche
das Brett

saw
la scie
die Säge

sandpaper
le papier de verre
das Sandpapier

log
la bûche
der Holzklotz

drill
la chignole
der Bohrer

sawdust
la sciure de bois
das Sägemehl

hacksaw
la scie à métaux
die Metallsäge

plane
le rabot
der Hobel

woodpecker
le pivert
der Specht

wood shavings
les copeaux
die Hobelspäne

screwdriver
le tournevis
der Schraubenzieher

screws
des vis
Schrauben

file
la lime
die Feile

pliers
les pinces
die Zange

jig saw
la scie à chantourner
die Spannsäge

14

bowsaw
la scie à bûches
die Bocksäge

trowel
la truelle
die Maurerkelle

hoe
une houe
die Mörtelhacke

bricklayer
le maçon
der Maurer

brick
la brique
der Ziegelstein

wall
le mur
die Mauer

cement
le mortier
der Mörtel

painter
le peintre
en bâtiment
der Anstreicher

paint brush
la brosse
die Malerbürste

timber
le bois de construction
das Bauholz

saw horse
le chevalet de sciage
der Sägebock

ball of twine
une pelote de ficelle
ein Bindfadenknäuel

paint
la peinture
die Farbe

barrel
le tonneau
das Faß

tack
une punaise
ein Stift

hammer
le marteau
der Hammer

hatchet
une hache
das Beil

rulers
des mètres
Zollstöcke

jackknife
le canif
das Taschenmesser

tool box
la boîte à outils
der Werkzeugkasten

putty knife
le couteau
à enduire
der Spachtel

shovel
la pelle
die Schaufel

bolt
le boulon
der Bolzen

nut
un écrou
eine Mutter

square
une équerre
das Winkelmaß

earth
la terre
die Erde

adjustable spanner
la clef à molette
der Engländer

compass
le compas
der Zirkel

wheelbarrow
la brouette
der Schubkarren

pick axe
la pioche
die Spitzhacke

glue
la colle
der Leim

15

weather cock
la girouette
der Wetterhahn

scarecrow
un épouvantail
eine Vogelscheuche

crow
une corneille
eine Krähe

plough
la charrue
der Pflug

field
le champ
der Acker

tractor
le tracteur
der Traktor

hayloft
le grenier à foin
der Heuboden

barn
la grange
die Scheune

goat
la chèvre
die Ziege

stable
une étable
der Stall

milk churn
le bidon de lait
die Milchkanne

tin can
la boîte de conserve
die Blechdose

pail
le seau
der Eimer

truck
la camionnette
der Lastwagen

cart
le chariot
der Wagen

hen
la poule
die Henne

cock
le coq
der Hahn

pigsty
la porcherie
der Schweinestall

chick
le poussin
das Küken

dog kennel
une niche
eine Hundehütte

16

haystack
la meule de foin
der Heuhaufen

cow
la vache
die Kuh

apple tree
le pommier
der Apfelbaum

farmhouse
la ferme
das Bauernhaus

water pump
la pompe
die Pumpe

meadow
le pré
die Wiese

fence
la clôture
der Zaun

horse
le cheval
das Pferd

sheep
le mouton
das Schaf

apple
la pomme
der Apfel

grass
herbe
das Gras

clothes-line
la corde à linge
die Wäscheleine

clothes basket
le panier à linge
der Wäschekorb

FARMER BEAR'S FARM

Farmer Bear has a very busy farm.
What is Mrs Bear doing? What is the horse doing?
What is the duck doing?

What is the scarecrow
supposed to be doing? He is
not doing it, is he?

FRESH
HONEY
AND
EGGS

chicken house
le poulailler
der Hühnerstall

well
le puits
der Ziehbrunnen

duck pond
la mare aux canards
der Ententeich

duck
la cane
die Ente

ducklings
les canetons
die Entenküken

bee
une abeille
die Biene

pitchfork
la fourche
die Mistgabel

beehive
les ruches
der Bienenstock

17

weather instruments
les appareils météorologiques
die Wetterinstrumente

blimp
le dirigeable
der Zeppelin

control tower
la tour de contrôle
der Kontrollturm

microphone
le microphone
das Mikrophon

helicopter
un hélicoptère
der Hubschrauber

AT THE AIRPORT

The man in the control tower is talking
into his microphone. He is talking to the
handsome pilot by radio. He is telling him
that he will have nice weather on his flight.

baggage train
le chariot à bagages
der Gepäckwagen

waiting room
*la salle
d'attente*
der Warteraum

telescope
le téléscope
das Fernrohr

tourist
un touriste
ein Tourist

camera
un appareil photo
der Photoapparat

observation deck
le belvédère
die Aussichtsterrasse

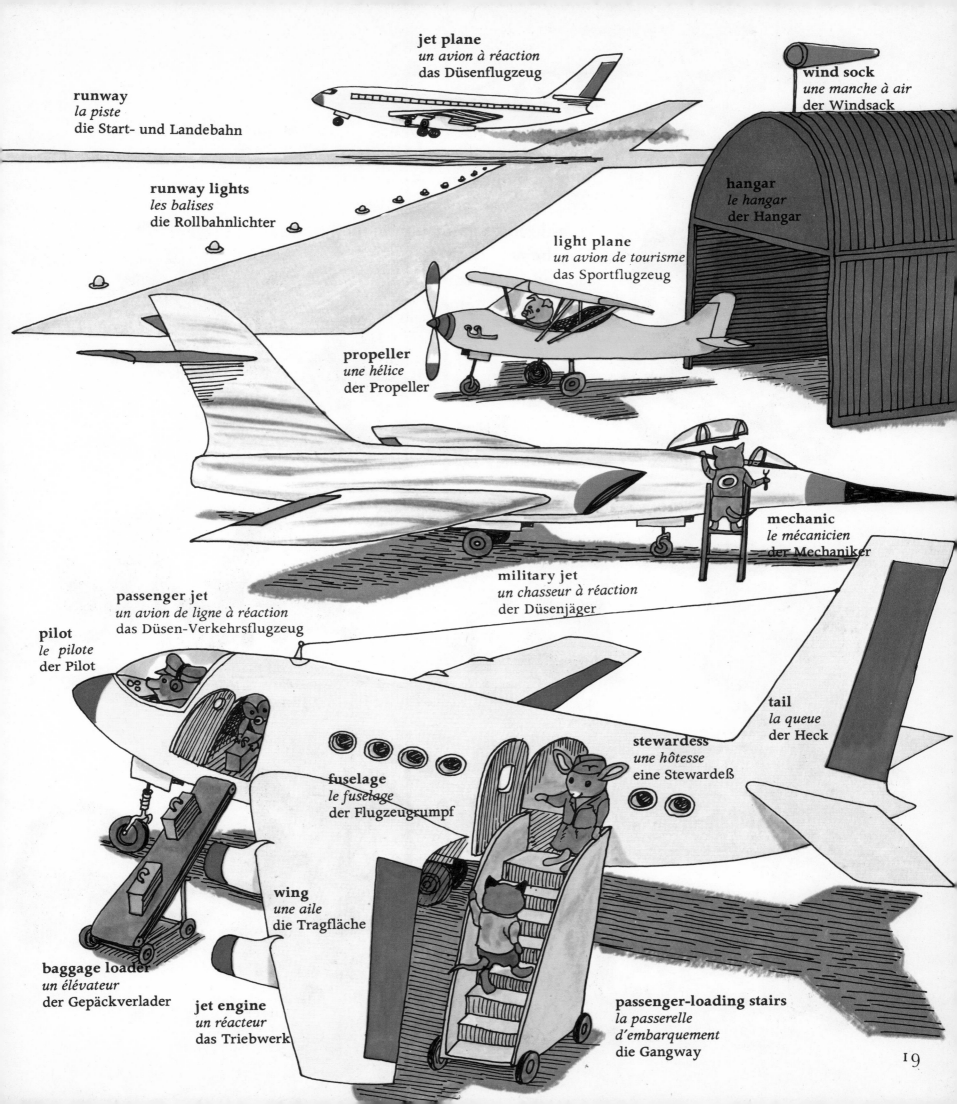

jet plane
un avion à réaction
das Düsenflugzeug

wind sock
une manche à air
der Windsack

runway
la piste
die Start- und Landebahn

runway lights
les balises
die Rollbahnlichter

hangar
le hangar
der Hangar

light plane
un avion de tourisme
das Sportflugzeug

propeller
une hélice
der Propeller

mechanic
le mécanicien
der Mechaniker

military jet
un chasseur à réaction
der Düsenjäger

passenger jet
un avion de ligne à réaction
das Düsen-Verkehrsflugzeug

pilot
le pilote
der Pilot

tail
la queue
der Heck

stewardess
une hôtesse
eine Stewardeß

fuselage
le fuselage
der Flugzeugrumpf

wing
une aile
die Tragfläche

baggage loader
un élévateur
der Gepäckverlader

jet engine
un réacteur
das Triebwerk

passenger-loading stairs
*la passerelle
d'embarquement*
die Gangway

19

TOYS

When you play with toys, it is more fun
if you share them with your friends.
When you play games you may win and
sometimes you may lose. Bear is a good sport.
He is losing a game but he might
win the next time.
Do you think he might
win the next game?

tricycle
le tricycle
das Dreirad

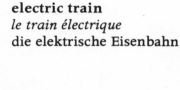

electric train
le train électrique
die elektrische Eisenbahn

teddy bear
un ours en peluche
der Teddybär

doll
la poupée
die Puppe

blocks
les cubes
die Holzklötzchen

lorry and loader
le camion et l'élévateur
der Lastwagen und der Auflader

Young Bear is losing.
L'ourson perd.
Das Bärchen verliert.

game
le jeu
das Spiel

Little Rabbit is winning.
Le petit lapin gagne.
Das Häschen gewinnt.

building set
un jeu de construction
die Bauelemente

20

castle
le fort
die Burg

croquet
le croquet
das Krocket

toy soldiers
les soldats de plomb
die Spielzeugsoldaten

tea set
le service à thé
das Teeservice

robot
le robot
der Roboter

racing car
une voiture de course
das Rennauto

typewriter
la machine à écrire
die Schreibmaschine

rocking horse
le cheval à bascule
das Schaukelpferd

Piglet is winning.
Le cochonnet gagne.
Das Schweinchen gewinnt.

bean bags
le jeu des sacs de haricots
das Bohnensackspiel

doll's house
la maison de poupée
das Puppenhaus

bow and arrow
un arc et une flèche
Pfeil und Bogen

scooter
la trottinette
der Roller

glider
le planeur
das Segelflugzeug

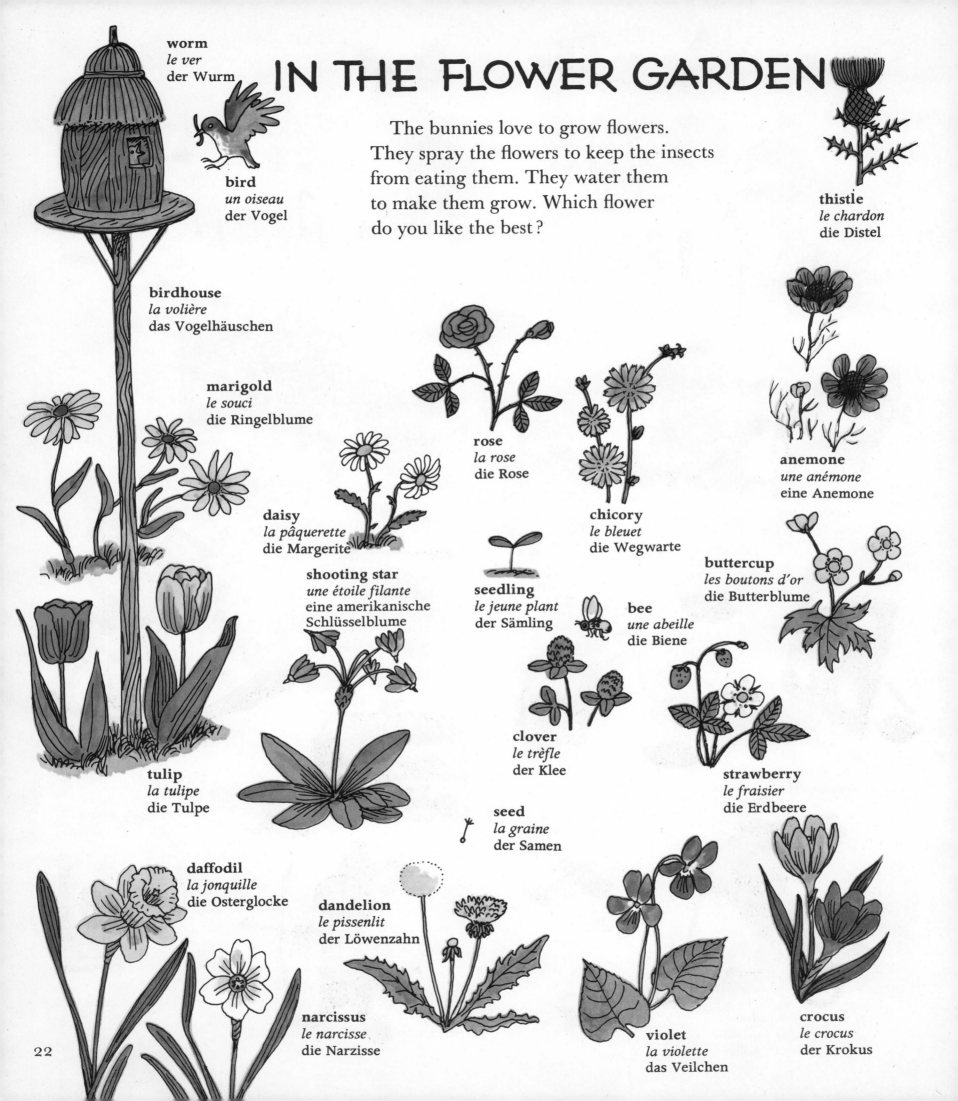

IN THE FLOWER GARDEN

worm
le ver
der Wurm

bird
un oiseau
der Vogel

The bunnies love to grow flowers.
They spray the flowers to keep the insects
from eating them. They water them
to make them grow. Which flower
do you like the best?

thistle
le chardon
die Distel

birdhouse
la volière
das Vogelhäuschen

marigold
le souci
die Ringelblume

rose
la rose
die Rose

anemone
une anémone
eine Anemone

daisy
la pâquerette
die Margerite

chicory
le bleuet
die Wegwarte

shooting star
une étoile filante
eine amerikanische
Schlüsselblume

seedling
le jeune plant
der Sämling

bee
une abeille
die Biene

buttercup
les boutons d'or
die Butterblume

clover
le trèfle
der Klee

strawberry
le fraisier
die Erdbeere

tulip
la tulipe
die Tulpe

seed
la graine
der Samen

daffodil
la jonquille
die Osterglocke

dandelion
le pissenlit
der Löwenzahn

narcissus
le narcisse
die Narzisse

violet
la violette
das Veilchen

crocus
le crocus
der Krokus

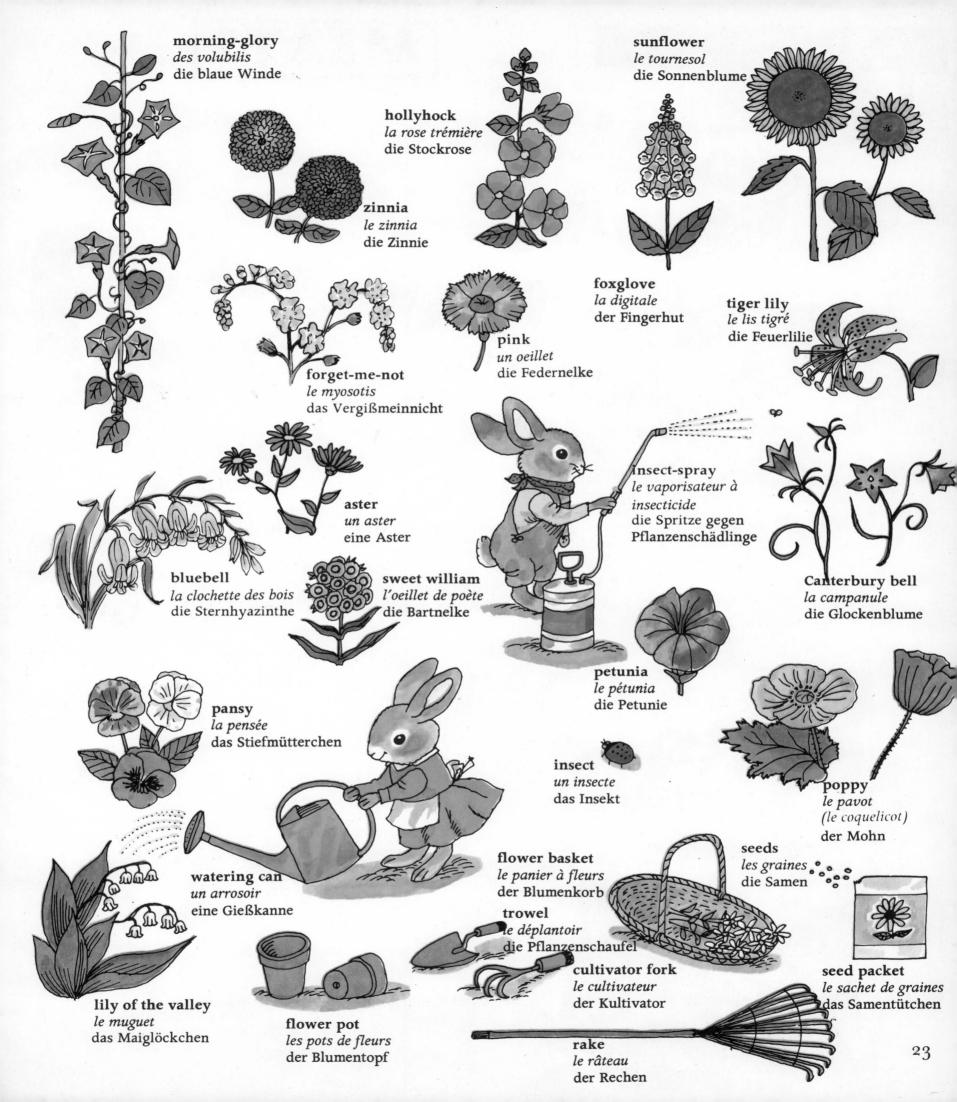

morning-glory
des volubilis
die blaue Winde

hollyhock
la rose trémière
die Stockrose

sunflower
le tournesol
die Sonnenblume

zinnia
le zinnia
die Zinnie

foxglove
la digitale
der Fingerhut

tiger lily
le lis tigré
die Feuerlilie

forget-me-not
le myosotis
das Vergißmeinnicht

pink
un oeillet
die Federnelke

aster
un aster
eine Aster

insect-spray
le vaporisateur à insecticide
die Spritze gegen Pflanzenschädlinge

bluebell
la clochette des bois
die Sternhyazinthe

sweet william
l'oeillet de poète
die Bartnelke

Canterbury bell
la campanule
die Glockenblume

pansy
la pensée
das Stiefmütterchen

petunia
le pétunia
die Petunie

insect
un insecte
das Insekt

poppy
le pavot
(le coquelicot)
der Mohn

watering can
un arrosoir
eine Gießkanne

flower basket
le panier à fleurs
der Blumenkorb

seeds
les graines
die Samen

trowel
le déplantoir
die Pflanzenschaufel

cultivator fork
le cultivateur
der Kultivator

seed packet
le sachet de graines
das Samentütchen

lily of the valley
le muguet
das Maiglöckchen

flower pot
les pots de fleurs
der Blumentopf

rake
le râteau
der Rechen

23

hook
le crochet
der Haken

ham
le jambon
der Schinken

saw
la scie
die Säge

scales
la balance
die Waage

MEATS

wrapping paper
le papier d'emballage
das Einwickelpapier

string
la ficelle
der Bindfaden

pickle barrel
le tonneau à cornichons
das Gurkenfaß

meat cleaver
le couperet
das Hackmesser

salami
le salami
die Salami

sausages
les saucisses
die Würstchen

mince
le steak haché
gehacktes Fleisch

fish
le poisson
der Fisch

dustbin
la poubelle
der Mülleimer

bacon
le bacon
der Speck

chop
la côtelette
das Kotelett

steak
une entrecôte
das Steak

trolley
le chariot
das Wägelchen

sawdust
la sciure de bois
das Sägemehl

AT THE SUPERMARKET

Mrs Pig is buying groceries for her family.
What would you like to buy the next time
you go to the market?
Would you like to buy a pickle?

books
les livres
Bücher

customer
une cliente
eine Kundin

orange juice
le jus d'orange
der Orangensaft

milk
le lait
die Milch

raisins
les raisins secs
die Rosinen

money
de l'argent
das Geld

handbag
le sac à main
die Handtasche

eggs
les oeufs
die Eier

butter
le beurre
die Butter

cashier
la caissière
die Kassiererin

ice cream
la glace
das Eis

cash register
la caisse enregistreuse
die Regestrierkasse

24

FRUITS

pineapple
un ananas
eine Ananas

apples
les pommes
die Äpfel

oranges
les oranges
die Orangen

pears
les poires
die Birnen

grapefruit
les pamplemousses
die Pampelmusen

bananas
les bananes
die Bananen

grocer
un épicier
der Lebensmittelhändler

scales
la balance
die Waage

melons
les melons
die Melonen

grapes
le raisin
die Weintrauben

lemons
les citrons
die Zitronen

cherries
les cerises
die Kirschen

plums
les prunes
die Pflaumen

strawberries
les fraises
die Erdbeeren

raspberries
les framboises
die Himbeeren

bilberries
les myrtilles
die Heidelbeeren

VEGETABLES

peaches
les pêches
die Pfirsiche

watermelon
la pastèque
die Wassermelone

coconut
la noix de coco
die Kokosnuß

cabbage
le chou
der Kohl

cauliflower
le chou-fleur
der Blumenkohl

corn on the cob
un épi de maïs
der Maiskolben

lettuce
la laitue
der Salat

asparagus
les asperges
die Spargeln

peas
les petits pois
die Erbsen

celery
le céleri
die Staudensellerie

beans
les haricots verts
die Bohnen

tomatoes
les tomates
die Tomaten

spinach
les épinards
der Spinat

potatoes
les pommes de terre
die Kartoffeln

onions
les oignons
die Zwiebeln

beetroots
les betteraves
die roten Rüben

carrots
les carottes
die Mohrrüben

cucumbers
les concombres
die Gurken

turnip
le navet
die weiße Rübe

biscuits
les biscuits
die Kekse

sugar
le sucre
der Zucker

cereal
les flocons d'avoine
die Getreideflocken

spaghetti
les spaghetti
die Spaghetti

tinned food
les conserves
die Konserven

peanut butter
le beurre de cacahouètes
die Erdnußbutter

broom
le balai
der Besen

cheese
le fromage

salt
le sel
das Salz

dried apricots
les abricots secs
Getrocknete Aprikosen

baby food
les aliments pour bébé
die Babynahrung

bread
le pain
das Brot

jam
la confiture
die Marmelade

25

MEALTIME

Father Pig, Mother Pig, and Peter Pig love to eat. There is so much food on the table it is hard to find Peter. Can you find him?

carving knife and fork
le couteau et la fourchette à découper
das Tranchierbesteck

roast beef
le rôti de boeuf
das Roastbeef

meat platter
le plat à viande
die Fleischplatte

tablespoon
la cuiller à servir
der Eßlöffel

coffee pot
la cafetière
die Kaffeekanne

teapot
la théière
die Teekanne

salt
le sel
das Salz

pepper
le poivre
der Pfeffer

fork
la fourchette
die Gabel

dinner plate
une assiette
ein flacher Teller

glass
le verre
das Glas

cream jug
le pot à crème
das Sahnekännchen

cup
la tasse
die Tasse

knife
le couteau
das Messer

spoon
la cuiller
der Löffel

saucer
la soucoupe
die Untertasse

napkin
la serviette
die Serviette

sugar bowl
le sucrier
die Zuckerdose

turkey
la dinde
der Truthahn

cake
le gâteau
der Kuchen

milk jug
le pot à lait
die Milchkanne

stuffing
la farce
das Füllsel

baked potatoes
les pommes de terre en robe des champs
In der Schale überbackene Kartoffeln

green beans
les haricots verts
grüne Bohnen

pudding
le pudding
der Pudding

cranberry jelly
la gelée d'airelles
das Preiselbeergelee

mashed potatoes
la purée
der Kartoffelbrei

beetroots
les betteraves
rote Rüben

onions
les oignons
die Zwiebeln

ice cream
la glace
das Eis

peas
les petits pois
die Erbsen

butter
le beurre
die Butter

steak
une entrecôte
das Steak

soup
le potage
die Suppe

pie
la tarte
der Auflauf

salad
la salade
der Salat

white bread
le pain blanc
das Weißbrot

rolls
les petits pains
die Semmeln

rye bread
le pain de seigle
das Roggenbrot

27

funnel
la cheminée
der Schornstein

submarine
le sous-marin
das Unterseeboot

stern
la poupe
das Heck

ocean liner
le transatlantique
der Ozeandampfer

tug
le remorqueur
der Schlepper

bow
la proue
der Bug

police boat
la vedette de police
das Polizeiboot

barge
le chaland
der Schleppkahn

ferry boat
le transbordeur
die Fähre

pirate ship
le navire corsaire
das Piratenschiff

BOATS AND SHIPS

What do you see in the water which is not
a boat? It helps boats find
the place they want to go.

motor boat
le canot à moteur
das Motorboot

paddle
la pagaie
die Paddel

canoe
le canoë
das Kanu

kayak
le kayak
der Kajak

oar
la rame
das Ruder

rowing boat
la barque
das Ruderboot

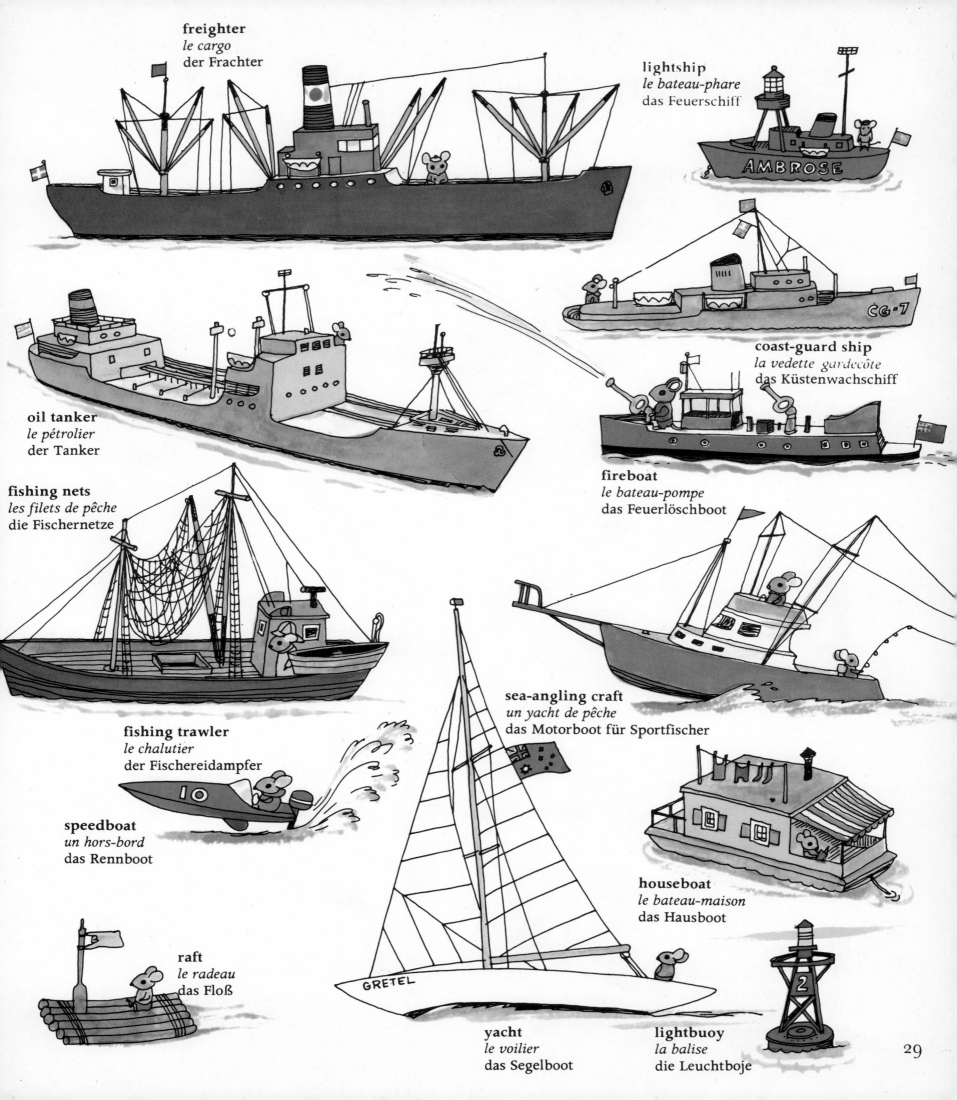

freighter
le cargo
der Frachter

lightship
le bateau-phare
das Feuerschiff

AMBROSE

CG-7

coast-guard ship
la vedette gardecôte
das Küstenwachschiff

oil tanker
le pétrolier
der Tanker

fireboat
le bateau-pompe
das Feuerlöschboot

fishing nets
les filets de pêche
die Fischernetze

fishing trawler
le chalutier
der Fischereidampfer

sea-angling craft
un yacht de pêche
das Motorboot für Sportfischer

speedboat
un hors-bord
das Rennboot

houseboat
le bateau-maison
das Hausboot

raft
le radeau
das Floß

GRETEL

yacht
le voilier
das Segelboot

lightbuoy
la balise
die Leuchtboje

29

KEEPING HEALTHY

Your doctor and your dentist are two of your
very best friends. They want to help you to stay
strong, healthy, and happy. Will you give your
doctor and dentist a great big smile the next
time you see them? How big can you smile?

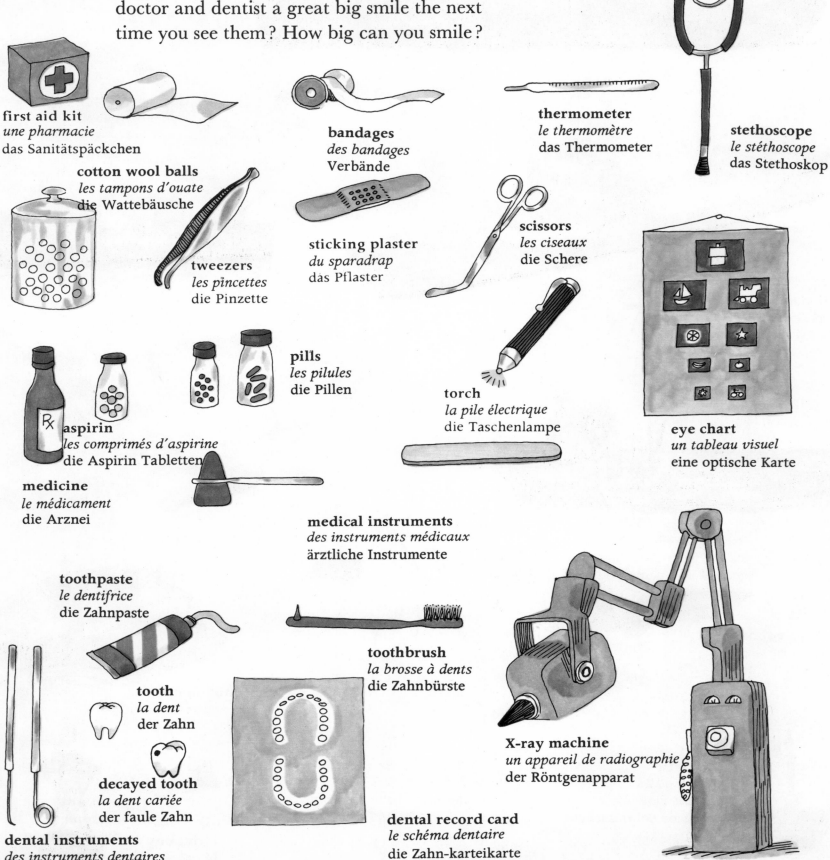

first aid kit
une pharmacie
das Sanitätspäckchen

bandages
des bandages
Verbände

thermometer
le thermomètre
das Thermometer

stethoscope
le stéthoscope
das Stethoskop

cotton wool balls
les tampons d'ouate
die Wattebäusche

sticking plaster
du sparadrap
das Pflaster

scissors
les ciseaux
die Schere

tweezers
les pincettes
die Pinzette

pills
les pilules
die Pillen

aspirin
les comprimés d'aspirine
die Aspirin Tabletten

torch
la pile électrique
die Taschenlampe

eye chart
un tableau visuel
eine optische Karte

medicine
le médicament
die Arznei

medical instruments
des instruments médicaux
ärztliche Instrumente

toothpaste
le dentifrice
die Zahnpaste

toothbrush
la brosse à dents
die Zahnbürste

tooth
la dent
der Zahn

decayed tooth
la dent cariée
der faule Zahn

X-ray machine
un appareil de radiographie
der Röntgenapparat

dental record card
le schéma dentaire
die Zahn-karteikarte

dental instruments
des instruments dentaires
zahnärztliche Instrumente

At the doctor's
chez le médecin
Beim Arzt

nurse
une infirmière
eine Krankenschwester

test tube
le tube à essai
das Reagenzglas

scales
la balance
die Waage

patient
le client
der Patient

doctor
le médecin
der Arzt

dental drill
la roulette
der Bohrer

At the dentist's
chez le dentiste
Beim Zahnarzt

dentist
le dentiste
der Zahnarzt

mouth-rinse bowl
le crachoir
das Becken

instrument table
la tablette
der Instrumententisch

glass
le verre
das Glas

dental unit
le bloc dentaire
die zahnärztliche Bohrmaschine

dentist's chair
le fauteuil dentaire
der Stuhl beim Zahnarzt

assistant
l'assistante
die Assistentin

31

THE BEAR TWINS GET DRESSED

Brother Bear woke up one cold, frosty morning.
He wanted to dress very warmly before
he went outside.

He yawned and got up out of bed.

He took off his pyjamas
and left them on the floor.
Naughty bear!

pyjama bottom
la culotte de pyjama
die Pyjamahose

pyjama top
la veste de pyjama
die Pyjamajacke

slippers
les pantoufles
die Hausschuhe

cap
la casquette
die Mütze

underwear
des sous-vêtements
die Unterwäsche

shirt
la chemise
das Hemd

trousers
la culotte
die Hose

overalls
la salopette
der Overall

tie
une cravatte
eine Krawatte

sweater
le chandail
der Pullover

socks
les chaussettes
die Socken

cap
un bonnet
eine Kappe

muffler
une écharpe
der Schal

plimsolls
des tennis
die Turnschuhe

gloves
des gants
die Handschuhe

jacket
un blouson
eine Jacke

overcoat
le manteau
der Mantel

raincoat
un imperméable
ein Regenmantel

and sou'wester
et un suroît
und ein Regenhut

As he was walking out of the front door
his Mother said, 'Don't forget

"Don't forget to put your boots on!"
«N'oublie pas de mettre tes bottes!»
,,Vergiß nicht, deine Stiefel anzuziehen!"

boots
les bottes
die Stiefel

Sister Bear got up out of bed.

She took off her pretty nightgown and put it away neatly. Nice bear!

nightgown
la chemise de nuit
das Nachthemd

petticoat
la combinaison
der Unterrock

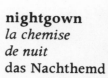

panties
la culotte
das Höschen

hair ribbon
un ruban
eine Haarschleife

blouse
le chemisier
die Bluse

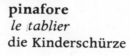

skirt
la jupe
der Rock

pinafore
le tablier
die Kinderschürze

stockings
les bas
die Strümpfe

ear muffs
les oreillettes
die Ohrenschützer

shoes
les souliers
die Schuhe

mittens
les moufles
die Fäustlinge

snow suit
un esquimau
der Rodelanzug

She put her handkerchief
Elle met son mouchoir
Sie steckte ihr Taschentuch

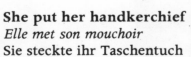
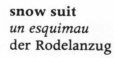

and her purse
et son porte-monnaie
und ihr Portemonnaie

in her handbag.
dans son sac.
in ihre Handtasche.

"Don't forget to put your boots on!"
«N'oublie pas de mettre tes bottes!»
„Vergiß nicht, deine Stiefel anzuziehen!"

33

deer
le cerf
der Hirsch

lion
le lion
der Löwe

elephant
un éléphant
der Elefant

tiger
le tigre
der Tiger

panda
le panda
der Katzenbär

monkeys
les singes
die Affen

brown bear
un ours brun
ein brauner Bär

gorilla
le gorille
der Gorilla

polar bear
un ours polaire
der Eisbär

34

buffalo
le buffle
der Buffel

camel
le chameau
das Kamel

zebra
le zèbre
das Zebra

zoo keeper
le gardien
der Zoowärter

sea lion
l'otiare
der Seelöwe

giraffe
la girafe
die Giraffe

leopard
le léopard
der Leopard

children's train
le train pour enfants
die Kinder-Eisenbahn

AT THE ZOO

Mr and Mrs Mouse took
their children to the zoo.
How will those children
ever be able to get
all those balloons
into their house tonight?
Which is your favourite animal
at the zoo?

rhinoceros
le rhinocéros
das Nashorn

hippopotamus
un hippopotame
das Nilpferd

DRAWING AND PAINTING

Everyone likes to draw and paint. Can you draw a ferris wheel? They are fun to ride on and they are fun to draw.

red
rouge
rot

violet
violet
lila

orange
orange
orange

blue
bleu
blau

yellow
jaune
gelb

green
vert
grün

ferris wheel
la grande roue
das Riesenrad

red
rouge
rot

yellow
jaune
gelb

blue
bleu
blau

yellow
jaune
gelb

make orange
donnent de l'orange
gibt orange

blue
bleu
blau

yellow
jaune
gelb

make green
donnent du vert
gibt grün

black
noir
schwarz

white
blanc
weiß

red
rouge
rot

blue
bleu
blau

makes violet
donnent du violet
gibt lila

red
rouge
rot

white
blanc
weiß

make pink
donnent du rose
gibt rosa

make grey
donnent du gris
gibt grau

water dish
le godet
der Wassernapf

red
rouge
rot

yellow
jaune
gelb

blue
bleu
blau

black
noir
schwarz

make brown
donnent du brun
gibt braun

paint brushes
les pinceaux
die Malpinsel

poster paint
la peinture pour affiches
die Plakatfarbe

rubber
la gomme
das Radiergummi

paint box
la boîte de peinture
der Malkasten

pens
les plumes
die Federn

pencil
le crayon
der Bleistift

ink
l'encre
die Tinte

crayons
les crayons de couleur
die Buntstifte

pastels
les crayons pastel
die Pastellstifte

poster
une affiche
das Plakat

mural painting
une fresque
eine Wandmalerei

artist
un artiste
der Künstler

dinosaur
le dinosaure
der Dinosaurier

scaffold
un échafaudage
das Gerüst

pastel sketch
une esquisse au pastel
eine Pastellskizze

canvas
la toile
die Leinwand

still-life model
une nature morte
das Stilleben

oil painting
*le tableau peint
à l'huile*
das Ölgemälde

palette
la palette
die Palette

pad of paper
le bloc de papier
der Zeichenblock

life model
le modèle
das Modell

smock
*une blouse
de peintre*
ein Malerkittel

paper
le papier
das Papier

watercolour
une aquarelle
das Aquarell

drawing
le dessin
die Zeichnung

37

NUMBERS

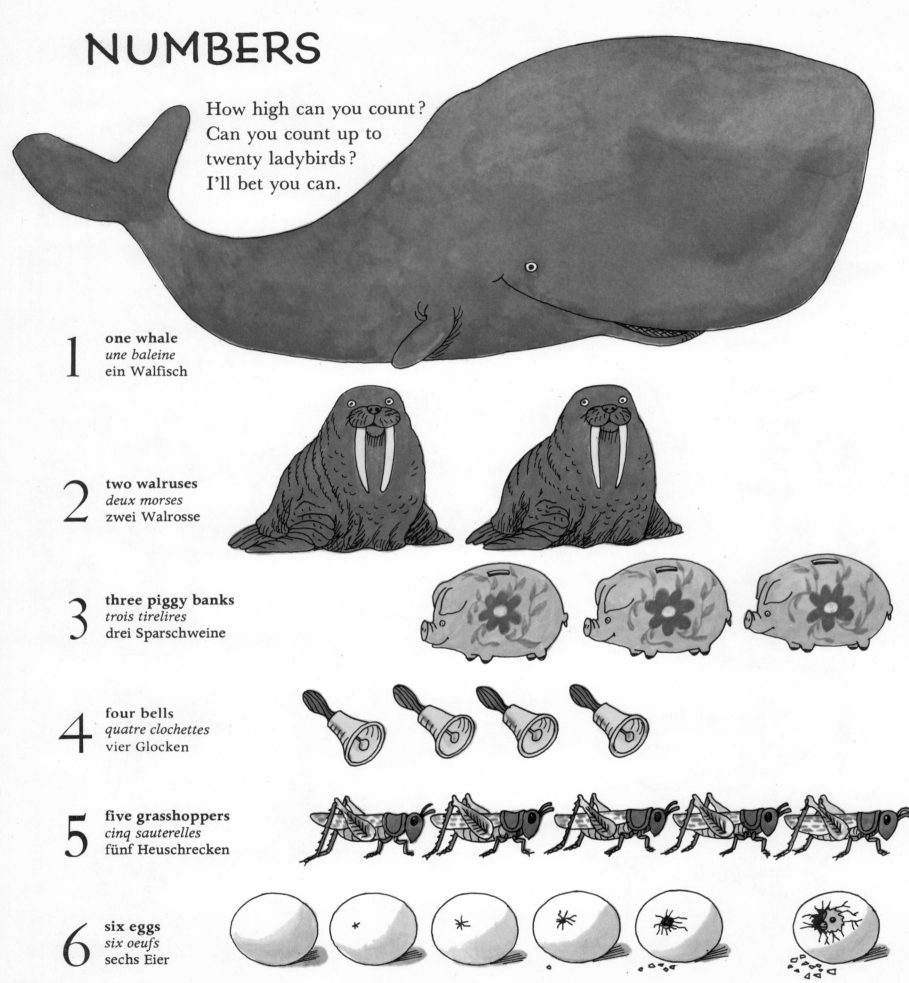

How high can you count?
Can you count up to
twenty ladybirds?
I'll bet you can.

1 **one whale**
une baleine
ein Walfisch

2 **two walruses**
deux morses
zwei Walrosse

3 **three piggy banks**
trois tirelires
drei Sparschweine

4 **four bells**
quatre clochettes
vier Glocken

5 **five grasshoppers**
cinq sauterelles
fünf Heuschrecken

6 **six eggs**
six oeufs
sechs Eier

7 **seven caterpillars**
sept chenilles
sieben Raupen

8 **eight reels**
huit bobines
acht Garnrollen

9 **nine spiders**
neuf araignées
neun Spinnen

10 **ten keys**
dix clefs
zehn Schlüssel

11 **eleven ants**
onze fourmis
elf Ameisen

12 **twelve rings**
douze bagues
zwölf Ringe

13 **thirteen gumdrops**
treize boules de gomme
dreizehn Gummibonbons

14 **fourteen leaves**
quatorze feuilles
vierzehn Blätter

15 **fifteen snowflakes**
quinze flocons de neige
fünfzehn Schneeflocken

16 **sixteen acorns**
seize glands
sechzehn Eicheln

17 **seventeen safety pins**
dix-sept épingles de nourrice
siebzehn Sicherheitsnadeln

18 **eighteen buttons**
dix-huit boutons
achtzehn Knöpfe

19 **nineteen beads**
dix-neuf perles
neunzehn Perlen

20 **twenty ladybirds**
vingt coccinelles
zwanzig Marienkäfer

MUSIC MAKING

The conductor leads the orchestra
by waving his baton. The musicians
are playing a very gay tune.
Which of the musical instruments do
you think you could learn to play?

bassoon
le basson
das Fagott

double bass
la contrebasse
der Kontrabaß

cello
le violoncelle
das Cello

oboe
le hautbois
die Oboe

clarinet
la clarinette
die Klarinette

flute
une flûte
die Flöte

piccolo
un piccolo
die Pikkoloflöte

baton
la baguette
der Taktstock

violin
le violon
die Violine

conductor
le chef d'orchestre
der Dirigent

grand piano
le piano à queue
der Flügel

viola
un alto
die Bratsche

podium
un pupitre
das Pult

notes
les notes
die Noten

kettle drums
les timbales
die Kesselpauken

snare drum
la caisse claire
die Trommel

bass drum
la grosse caisse
die Pauke

cymbals
les cymbales
die Becken

triangle
le triangle
der Triangel

French horn
le cor d'harmonie
das Waldhorn

trumpet
la trompette
die Trompete

tuba
le tuba
die Tuba

saxophone
le saxophone
das Saxophon

tambourine
le tambourin
das Tamburin

cornet
*le cornet
à pistons*
das Kornett

trombone
le trombone
die Posaune

banjo
le banjo
der Banjo

guitar
la guitare
die Gitarre

comb and tissue paper
*un peigne et du
papier de soie*
das Kammblasen

harp
une harpe
die Harfe

accordion
un accordéon
die Ziehharmonika

harmonica
un harmonica
die Mundharmonika

41

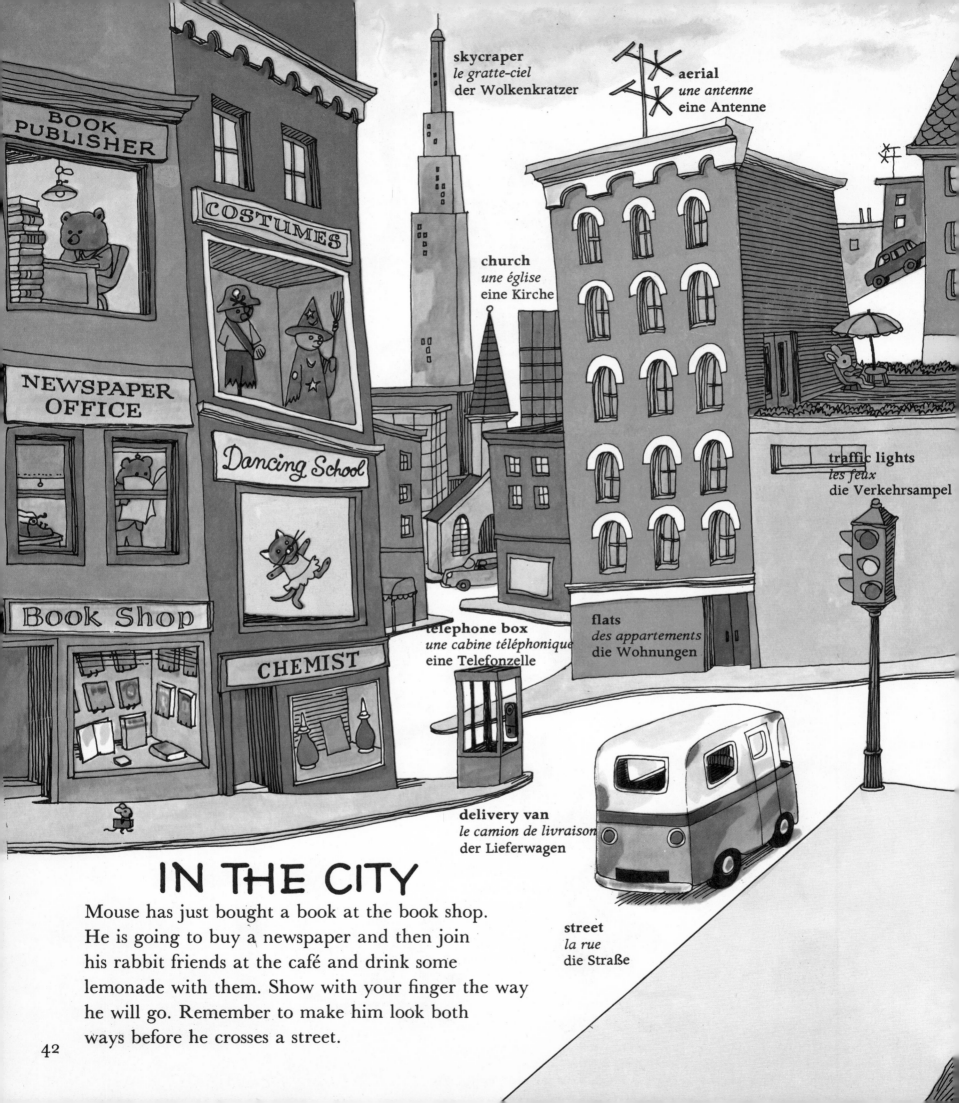

BOOK PUBLISHER

COSTUMES

NEWSPAPER OFFICE

Dancing School

Book Shop

CHEMIST

skycraper
le gratte-ciel
der Wolkenkratzer

aerial
une antenne
eine Antenne

church
une église
eine Kirche

traffic lights
les feux
die Verkehrsampel

telephone box
une cabine téléphonique
eine Telefonzelle

flats
des appartements
die Wohnungen

delivery van
le camion de livraison
der Lieferwagen

IN THE CITY

Mouse has just bought a book at the book shop.
He is going to buy a newspaper and then join
his rabbit friends at the café and drink some
lemonade with them. Show with your finger the way
he will go. Remember to make him look both
ways before he crosses a street.

street
la rue
die Straße

42

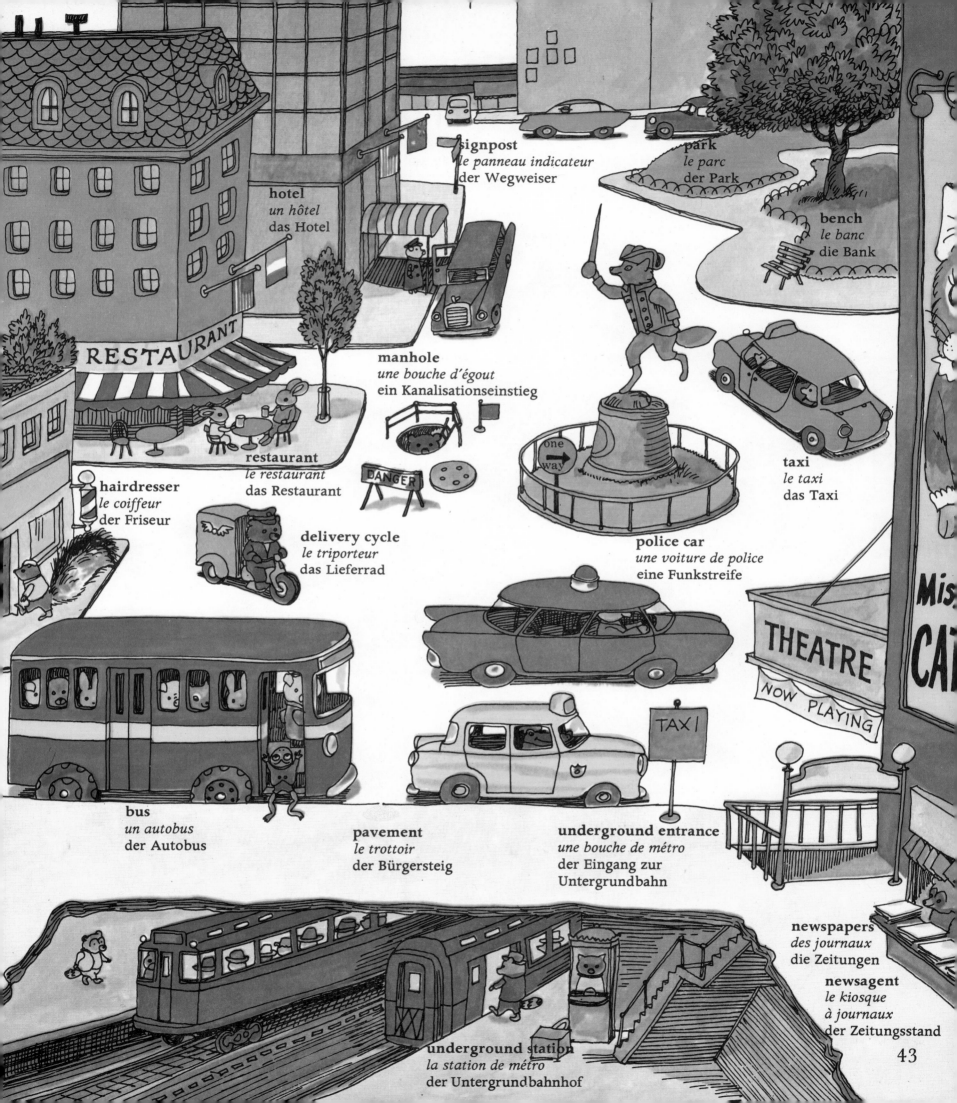

signpost
le panneau indicateur
der Wegweiser

park
le parc
der Park

hotel
un hôtel
das Hotel

bench
le banc
die Bank

RESTAURANT

manhole
une bouche d'égout
ein Kanalisationseinstieg

DANGER

taxi
le taxi
das Taxi

restaurant
le restaurant
das Restaurant

hairdresser
le coiffeur
der Friseur

one way

delivery cycle
le triporteur
das Lieferrad

police car
une voiture de police
eine Funkstreife

THEATRE

NOW PLAYING

Mis

CA

TAXI

bus
un autobus
der Autobus

pavement
le trottoir
der Bürgersteig

underground entrance
une bouche de métro
der Eingang zur
Untergrundbahn

newspapers
des journaux
die Zeitungen

newsagent
le kiosque
à journaux
der Zeitungsstand

underground station
la station de métro
der Untergrundbahnhof

43

radio tower
le relais de radiodiffusion
der Funkturm

A DRIVE IN THE COUNTRY

There are many things to see when you take a drive in the country. Can you see what the mountain climber has dropped out of his knapsack?

ocean
la mer
das Meer

island
une île
eine Insel

factory
une usine
eine Fabrik

lake
le lac
der See

tunnel
le tunnel
der Tunnel

petrol station
la station-service
die Tankstelle

petrol pump
la pompe à essence
die Zapfsäule

motorway
l'autoroute
die Autobahn

bridge
un pont
eine Brücke

brook
le ruisselet
das Bächlein

farm
la ferme
der Bauernhof

mill
le moulin
die Mühle

stream
le ruisseau
der Bach

waterfall
la chute d'eau
der Wasserfall

layby
un refuge
der Rastplatz

lighthouse
le phare
der Leuchtturm

lookout tower
le mirador
der Hochsitz

beach
la plage
der Strand

crane
la grue
der Kran

bay
la baie
die Bucht

trees
des arbres
die Bäume

harbour
le port
der Hafen

drawbridge
le pont basculant
die Zugbrücke

hill
la colline
der Hügel

village
le village
das Dorf

mountain
la montagne
der Berg

windmill
une éolienne
das Windrad

large river
le fleuve
der Strom

log cabin
le refuge
das Blockhaus

pond
un étang
der Teich

river
une rivière
der Fluß

mountain climber
un alpiniste
der Bergsteiger

forest
la forêt
der Wald

road
la route
die Landstraße

knapsack
le sac à dos
der Rucksack

cliff
la paroi
die Felswand

apple
une pomme
der Apfel

45

HOLIDAYS

Which holiday do you like best?
I bet you like them all.
Holidays are always very happy times,
aren't they? What did you get from
Santa Claus last Christmas?

New Year
le Nouvel An
Neujahr

St Valentine's Day
la Saint-Valentin
der Valentinstag

balloons
les ballons
die Ballons

Easter
Pâques
Ostern

Easter egg
l'oeuf de Pâques
das Osterei

Easter bunny
un lapin de Pâques
der Osterhase

chick
le poussin
das Küken

cake
le gâteau
der Kuchen

ice cream
la glace
das Eis

Birthday
Anniversaire
Geburtstag

The Carnival
Le carnaval
Der Karneval

bugle
le clairon
das Horn

fireworks
le feu d'artifice
das Feuerwerk

fife
le fifre
die Querpfeife

trumpet
la trompette
die Trompete

bass drum
la grosse caisse
die Pauke

drum
le tambour
die Trommel

ghost
le fantôme
das Gespenst

Hallowe'en
La veille de la Toussaint
Der Abend vor Allerheiligen

moon
la lune
der Mond

fancy dress
le déguisement
das Maskenkostüm

witch
la sorcière
die Hexe

broom
le balai
der Besen

black cat
le chat noir
die schwarze Katze

Christmas
Noël
Weihnachten

angel
un ange
der Engel

candle
la bougie
die Kerze

Christmas tree
un arbre de Noël
der Weihnachtsbaum

wreath
la couronne
der Kranz

holly
le houx
die Stechpalme

ornaments
les décorations
der Schmuck

fairy-lights
les lampions
die Lichter

beard
la barbe
der Bart

fireplace
la cheminée
der Kamin

sack
le sac
der Sack

Father Christmas
Le Père Noël
der Weihnachtsmann

present
le cadeau
das Geschenk

AT SCHOOL

School is fun. There are so many things we learn to do. Little Bear is learning how to find a lost glove.

pencil sharpener
le taille-crayon
der Bleistiftspitzer

chalk
la craie
die Kreide

blackboard rubber
une éponge
der Tafelreiniger

scissors
des ciseaux
die Schere

glue
la colle
der Leim

modelling clay
la pâte à modeler
das Plastilin

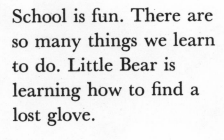

pencil
le crayon
der Bleistift

pen
le stylo
der Federhalter

ballpoint pen
le crayon à bille
der Kugelschreiber

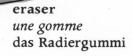

paper
des papiers
das Papier

notebook
un carnet de notes
das Notizbuch

ink
l'encre
die Tinte

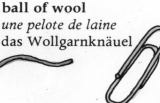

eraser
une gomme
das Radiergummi

milk
le lait
die Milch

biscuits
des biscuits
die Zwiebäcke

string
la ficelle
der Bindfaden

ball of wool
une pelote de laine
das Wollgarnknäuel

paper clip
le trombone
die Büroklammer

exercise book
un cahier
das Heft

storybook
un livre de lecture
das Lesebuch

drawing pins
des punaises
die Reißnägel

lost-clothing drawer
le tiroir aux objets perdus
Fundsachen in der Schublade

clock
la pendule
die Uhr

bell
la sonnette
die Klingel

blackboard
le tableau noir
die Tafel

calendar
le calendrier
der Kalender

teacher
un instituteur / une institutrice
der Lehrer / die Lehrerin

JANUARY

inkwell
l'encrier
das Tintenfaß

map
la carte
die Landkarte

map stand
le support
der Landkartenständer

wastepaper basket
une corbeille à papier
der Papierkorb

(girl) pupil
une élève
die Schülerin

(boy) pupil
un élève
der Schüler

desk
le pupitre
der Schreibtisch

classroom
la salle de classe
das Klassenzimmer

paper dolls
des bonhommes en papier
die Papierpuppen

headmaster
le directeur
der Rektor

49

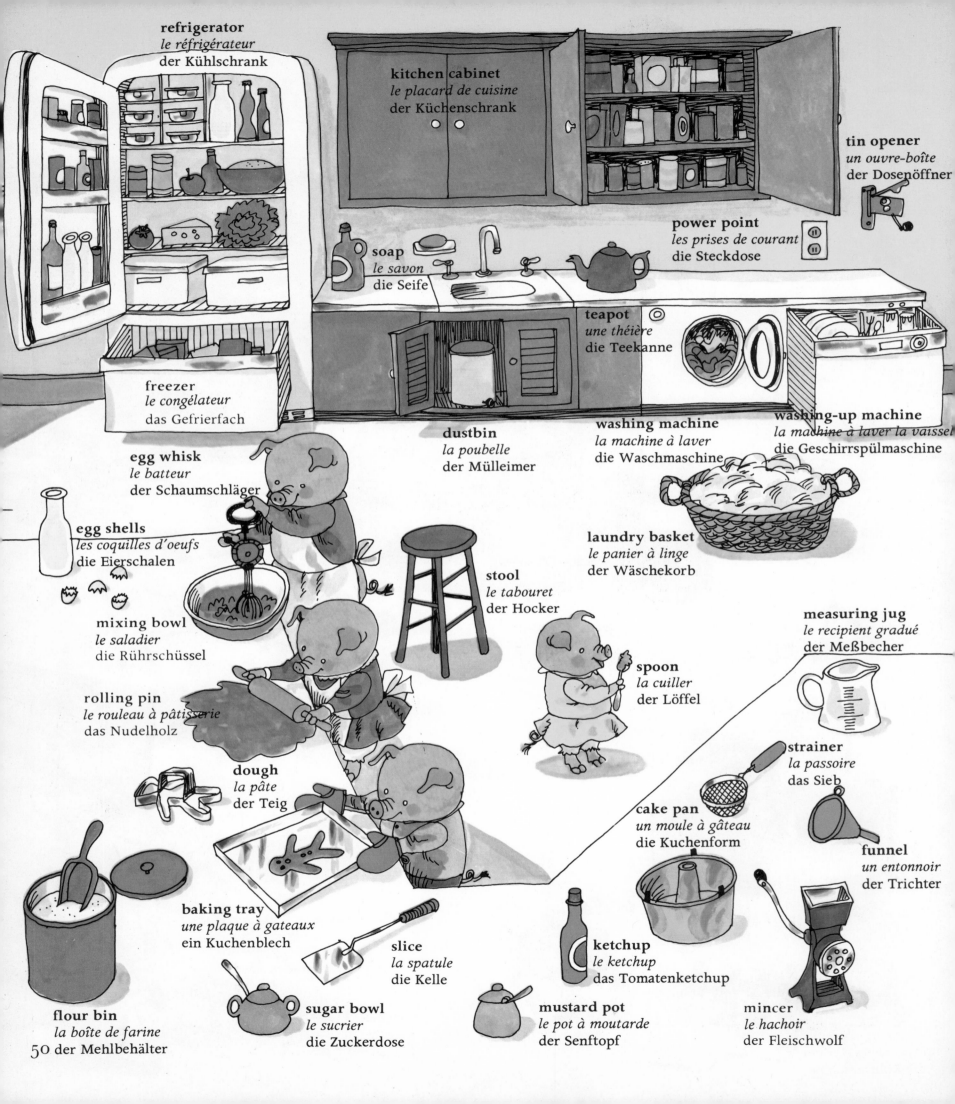

refrigerator
le réfrigérateur
der Kühlschrank

kitchen cabinet
le placard de cuisine
der Küchenschrank

tin opener
un ouvre-boîte
der Dosenöffner

power point
les prises de courant
die Steckdose

soap
le savon
die Seife

teapot
une théière
die Teekanne

freezer
le congélateur
das Gefrierfach

dustbin
la poubelle
der Mülleimer

washing machine
la machine à laver
die Waschmaschine

washing-up machine
la machine à laver la vaisselle
die Geschirrspülmaschine

egg whisk
le batteur
der Schaumschläger

egg shells
les coquilles d'oeufs
die Eierschalen

mixing bowl
le saladier
die Rührschüssel

rolling pin
le rouleau à pâtisserie
das Nudelholz

dough
la pâte
der Teig

stool
le tabouret
der Hocker

laundry basket
le panier à linge
der Wäschekorb

spoon
la cuiller
der Löffel

measuring jug
le recipient gradué
der Meßbecher

strainer
la passoire
das Sieb

cake pan
un moule à gâteau
die Kuchenform

funnel
un entonnoir
der Trichter

baking tray
une plaque à gateaux
ein Kuchenblech

slice
la spatule
die Kelle

ketchup
le ketchup
das Tomatenketchup

flour bin
la boîte de farine
50 der Mehlbehälter

sugar bowl
le sucrier
die Zuckerdose

mustard pot
le pot à moutarde
der Senftopf

mincer
le hachoir
der Fleischwolf

broom cupboard
le débarras
der Besenschrank

feather duster
le plumeau
der Staubwedel

egg timer
un sablier
eine Eieruhr

shelf
une étagère
das Küchenbord

coffee pot
la cafetière
die Kaffeekanne

fly swatter
la tapette à mouches
der Fliegenwedel

dust pan
la pelle
à poussière
die Kehrschaufel

kettle
la bouilloire
der Wasserkessel

stove
la cuisinière
der Herd

broom
le balai
der Besen

mop
le balai
à franges
der Mop

vacuum cleaner
un aspirateur
der Staubsauger

oven
le four
der Backofen

iron
le fer à repasser
das Bügeleisen

IN THE KITCHEN

All the little piglets like to help
their mother in the kitchen. They are
making good things to eat. What is
Mother Pig putting into the oven?

ironing board
la planche à repasser
das Bügelbrett

teaspoon
la petite cuiller
der Teelöffel

tablespoon
la cuiller à servir
der Eßlöffel

double-boiler
la marmite à vapeur
der Dampfkochtopf

blender
le mixer
das Mix-Gerät

pestle
le pilon
der Stößel

toaster
le grille-pain
der Toaströster

soup spoon
la cuiller à soupe
der Suppenlöffel

ladle
une louche
eine Schöpfkelle

colander
la passoire
der Seiher

mortar
le mortier
der Mörser

corkscrew
le tire-bouchon
der Korkenzieher

saucepan
la casserole
der Kochtopf

pepper mill
un moulin à poivre
eine Pfeffermühle

matches
les allumettes
die Streichhölzer

cutting board
la planche
à découper
das Holzbrettchen

measuring spoons
les mesures
die Maßlöffel

carving knife and fork
le couteau et la
fourchette à découper
das Tranchierbesteck

potato masher
le presse-purée
der Kartoffelstampfer

salt
le sel
das Salz

electric mixer
le batteur électrique
die Rührmaschine

cookery book
un livre de cuisine
das Kochbuch

51

BUILDINGS

Buildings are used for different things. You wouldn't kick a ball in a museum or a cathedral. Where is a good place to kick a football? What do people do in the other buildings?

skyscraper
le gratte-ciel
der Wolkenkratzer

fort
le fort
das Fort

tower
la tour
der Turm

museum
le musée
das Museum

triumphal arch
un arc de triomphe
der Triumphbogen

school
une école
eine Schule

pyramid
la pyramide
die Pyramide

stadium
le stade
das Stadion

windmill
le moulin à vent
die Windmühle

mosque
la mosquée
die Moschee

cathedral
la cathédrale
der Dom

church
une église
eine Kirche

library
la bibliothèque
die Bibliothek

factory
une usine
eine Fabrik

53

WHEN YOU GROW UP

What would you like to be when you are bigger? Would you like to be a good cook like your father? Or would you like to be a doctor or a nurse?

What would you like to be?

policeman
l'agent de police
der Polizist

fireman
le pompier
der Feuerwehrmann

sailor
le marin
der Matrose

nurse
une infirmière
eine Krankenschwester

milkman
le laitier
der Milchmann

farmer
le fermier
der Bauer

doctor
le médecin
der Arzt

carpenter
le menuisier
der Tischler

musician
un musicien
ein Musiker

cowboy
un cow-boy
ein Cowboy

secretary
la secrétaire
die Sekretärin

butcher
le boucher
der Fleischer

dentist
le dentiste
der Zahnarzt

cook
un cuisinier
ein Koch

54

singer
la chanteuse
die Sängerin

artist
un artiste peintre
ein Maler

pilot
le pilote
der Pilot

fisherman
le pêcheur
der Fischer

lorry driver
le camionneur
der Lastwagenfahrer

teacher
une institutrice
eine Lehrerin

garage mechanic
le mécanicien
der Automechaniker

train conductor
le contrôleur
de chemin de fer
der Zugschaffner

shopkeeper
le commerçant
der Kaufmann

soldier
le soldat
der Soldat

dancer
la danseuse
die Tänzerin

librarian
une bibliothécaire
eine Bibliothekarin

father
le père
der Vater

mother
la mère
die Mutter

55

THE ALPHABET

The alligator is eating an apple.
The goose is wearing gloves.
What is the Indian eating?

G   **GOOSE**
oie
Gans

A   **ALLIGATOR**
alligator
Alligator

H   **HEART**
coeur
Herz

B   **BEAR**
ours
Bär

I   **ICE CREAM**
glace
Eis

C   **CAT**
chat
Katze

D   **DOG**
chien
Hund

J   **JUG**
pot
Krug

E   **EGG**
oeuf
Ei

K   **KANGAROO**
kangourou
Känguruh

F   **FISH**
poisson
Fisch

L   **LETTER**
lettre
Brief

M   **MOUSE**
souris
Maus

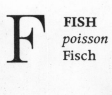

N
NUT
noix
Nuß

O
OWL
hibou
Eule

P
PRESENT
cadeau
Geschenk

Q
QUEEN
reine
Königin

R
RUG
carpette
Vorleger

S
SPIDER
araignée
Spinne

T
TORTOISE
tortue
Schildkröte

U
UMBRELLA
parapluie
Regenschirm

V
VASE
vase
Vase

W
WALRUS
morse
Walroß

X
XYLOPHONE
xylophone
Xylophon

Y
YARN
laine filée
Garn

Z
ZIP
fermeture éclair
Reißverschluß

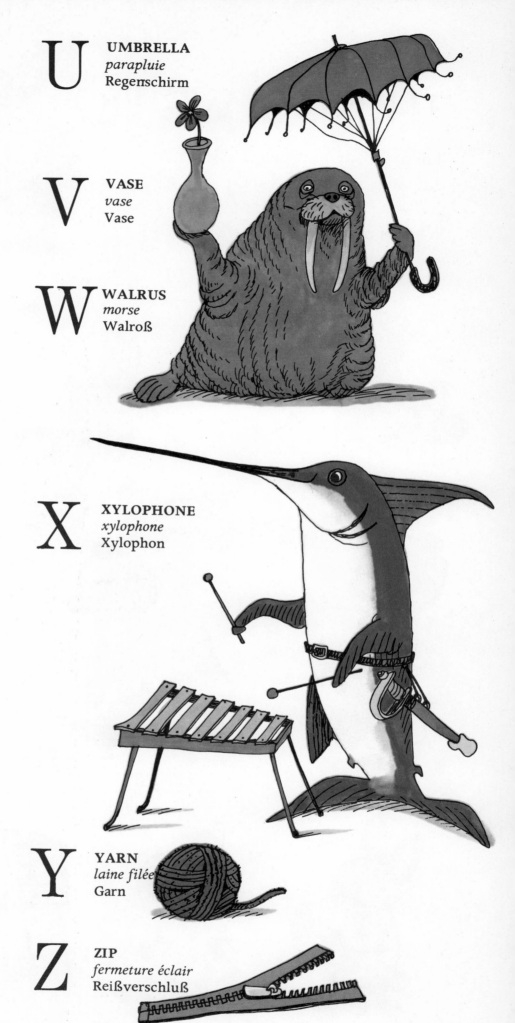

THINGS WE DO

There are many things
that we can do. And there
are some things we cannot do.
What is one thing we can't do?
Look and see.

dig
creuser
graben

blow
souffler
blasen

build
construire
bauen

break
casser
zerbrechen

sleep
dormir
schlafen

wake up
s'éveiller
aufwachen

walk
marcher
gehen

run
courir
laufen

stand
se tenir debout
stehen

sit
être assis
sitzen

read
lire
lesen

watch
regarder
zuschauen

write
écrire
schreiben

58

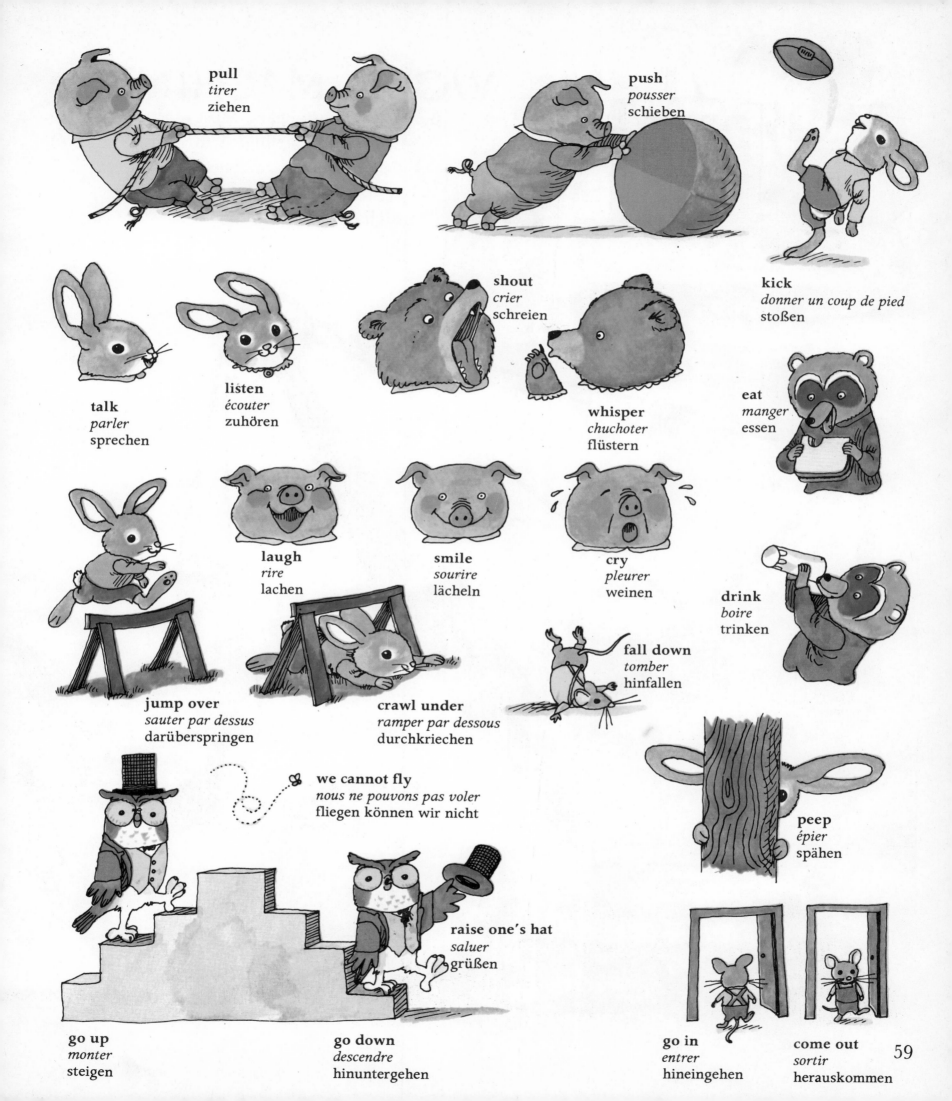

pull
tirer
ziehen

push
pousser
schieben

kick
donner un coup de pied
stoßen

talk
parler
sprechen

listen
écouter
zuhören

shout
crier
schreien

whisper
chuchoter
flüstern

eat
manger
essen

laugh
rire
lachen

smile
sourire
lächeln

cry
pleurer
weinen

drink
boire
trinken

jump over
sauter par dessus
darüberspringen

crawl under
ramper par dessous
durchkriechen

fall down
tomber
hinfallen

we cannot fly
nous ne pouvons pas voler
fliegen können wir nicht

peep
épier
spähen

raise one's hat
saluer
grüßen

go up
monter
steigen

go down
descendre
hinuntergehen

go in
entrer
hineingehen

come out
sortir
herauskommen

59

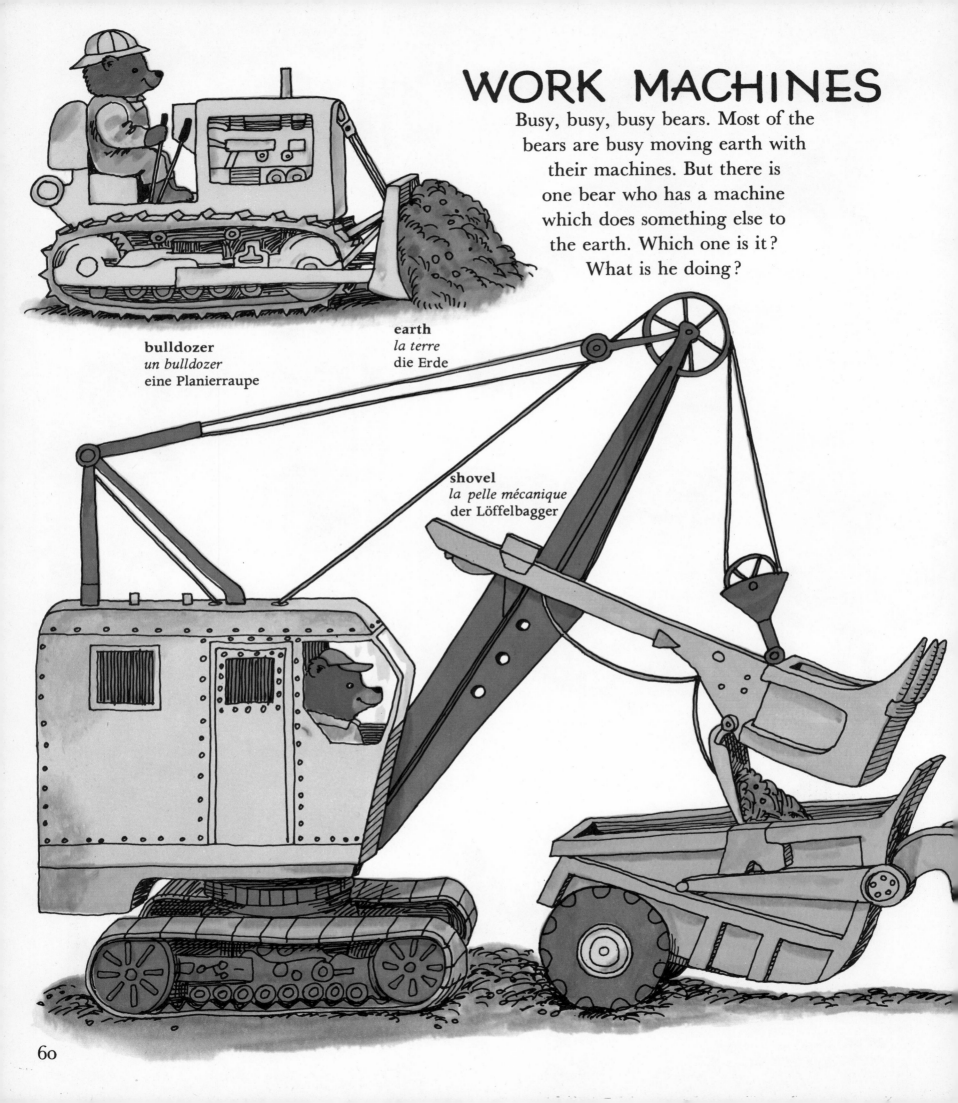

WORK MACHINES

Busy, busy, busy bears. Most of the bears are busy moving earth with their machines. But there is one bear who has a machine which does something else to the earth. Which one is it? What is he doing?

bulldozer
un bulldozer
eine Planierraupe

earth
la terre
die Erde

shovel
la pelle mécanique
der Löffelbagger

60

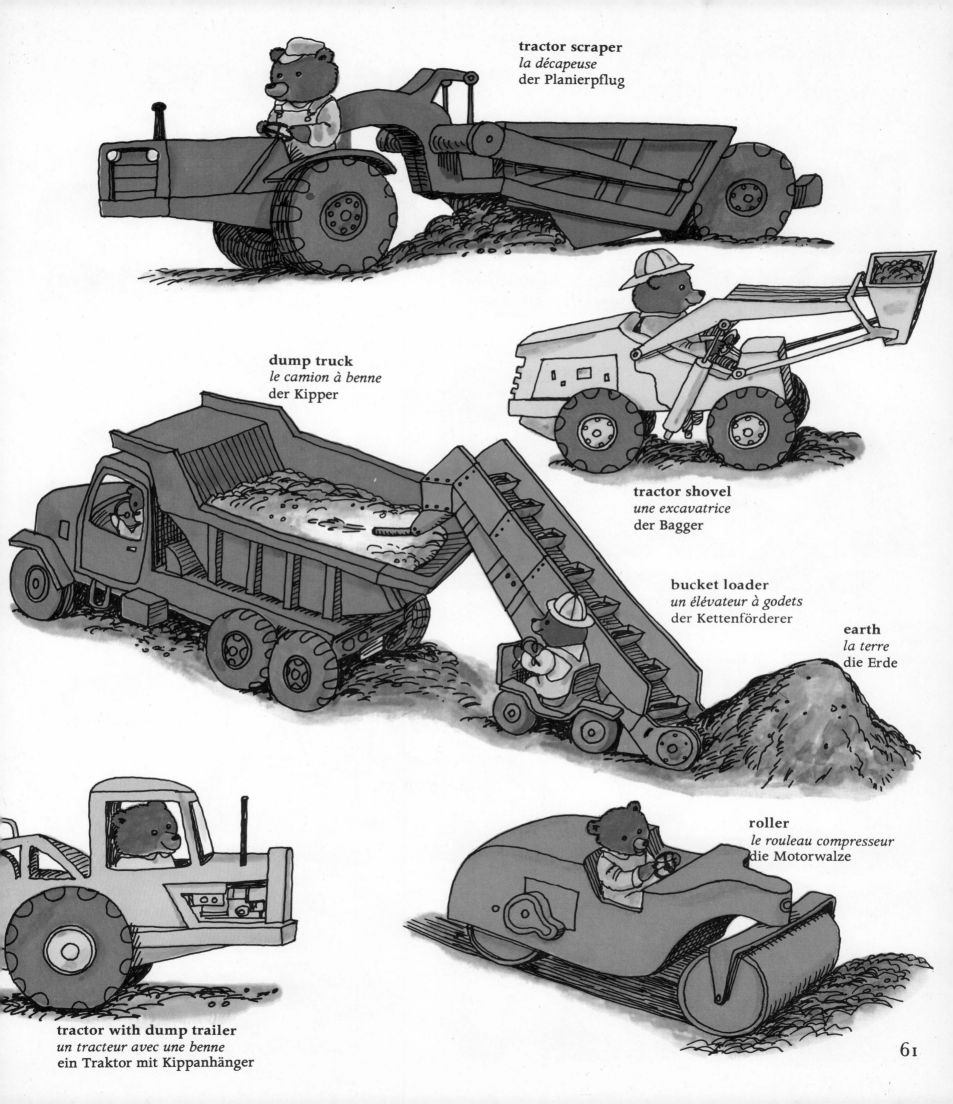

tractor scraper
la décapeuse
der Planierpflug

dump truck
le camion à benne
der Kipper

tractor shovel
une excavatrice
der Bagger

bucket loader
un élévateur à godets
der Kettenförderer

earth
la terre
die Erde

roller
le rouleau compresseur
die Motorwalze

tractor with dump trailer
un tracteur avec une benne
ein Traktor mit Kippanhänger

61

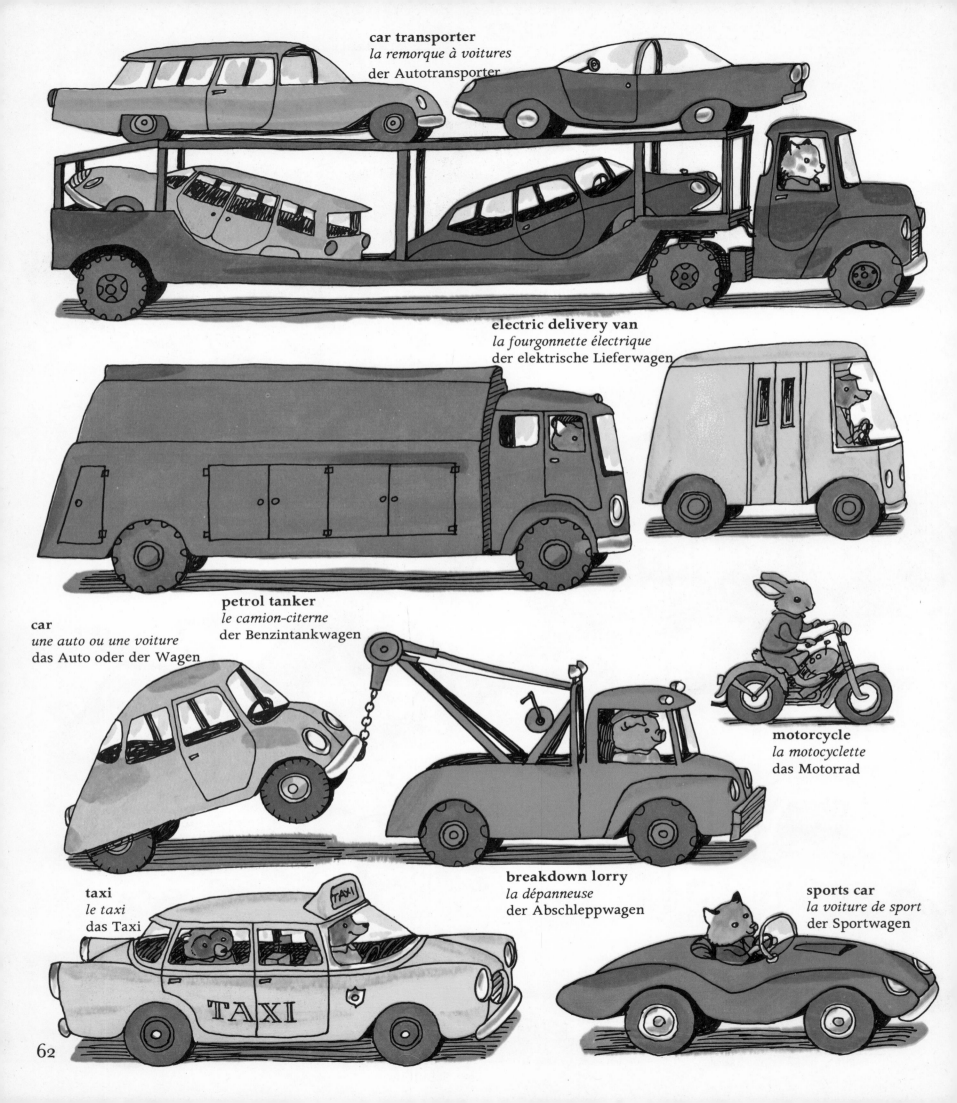

car transporter
la remorque à voitures
der Autotransporter

electric delivery van
la fourgonnette électrique
der elektrische Lieferwagen

car
une auto ou une voiture
das Auto oder der Wagen

petrol tanker
le camion-citerne
der Benzintankwagen

motorcycle
la motocyclette
das Motorrad

breakdown lorry
la dépanneuse
der Abschleppwagen

taxi
le taxi
das Taxi

sports car
la voiture de sport
der Sportwagen

62

WORLD-WIDE REMOVALS

heavy lorry
le camion de déménagement
der Lastkraftwagen

dustcart
le camion de voirie
der Müllwagen

CARS AND LORRIES

Down the street go the
cars and lorries.
But look! Some of the
cars don't have drivers.
Which cars have no drivers?

boat trailer
la remorque à bateau
der Bootswagen

station wagon
le break
der Kombiwagen

scooter
le scooter
der Motorroller

SCHOOL BUS

vintage car
une voiture ancienne
ein antiques Auto

school bus
le car de ramassage scolaire
der Schulbus

63

HOTEL

GENERAL STORE
COWBOY SUITS

BOOTS

BANK

TOWN HALL

street-lamp
le réverbère
die Straßenlaterne

hitching post
la barre d'attache
der Anbindepfosten

gold miner
un chercheur d'or
ein Goldgräber

donkey
le bourricot
der Packesel

money box
le coffre
die Geldkassette

cowboy
un cow-boy
ein Cowboy

sheriff
le shériff
der Sheriff

locomotive
une locomotive
eine Lokomotive

headlight
le fanal
der Scheinwerfer

stagecoach
la diligence
die Postkutsche

wheel
la roue
das Rad

BUFFALO BILL

OUT WEST

Indian is coming to town to buy a horse for his squaw to ride. Why do you think it would be nice for her to have a horse to ride?

covered wagon
le fourgon bâché
der Planwagen

saddle
la selle
der Sattel

dust
la poussière
der Staub

oxen
les boeufs
die Ochsen

Indian
un Indien
ein Indianer

papoose
un bébé indien
ein Indianerbaby

horseshoe
le fer à cheval
das Hufeisen

squaw
une squaw
eine Indianerfrau

barrel
la barrique
das Faß

lasso
le lasso
das Lasso

cattle truck
le wagon à bestiaux
der Viehwagen

tender
le tender
der Tender

cattle
le bétail
das Vieh

corral
un enclos
der Pferch

horse
le cheval
das Pferd

65

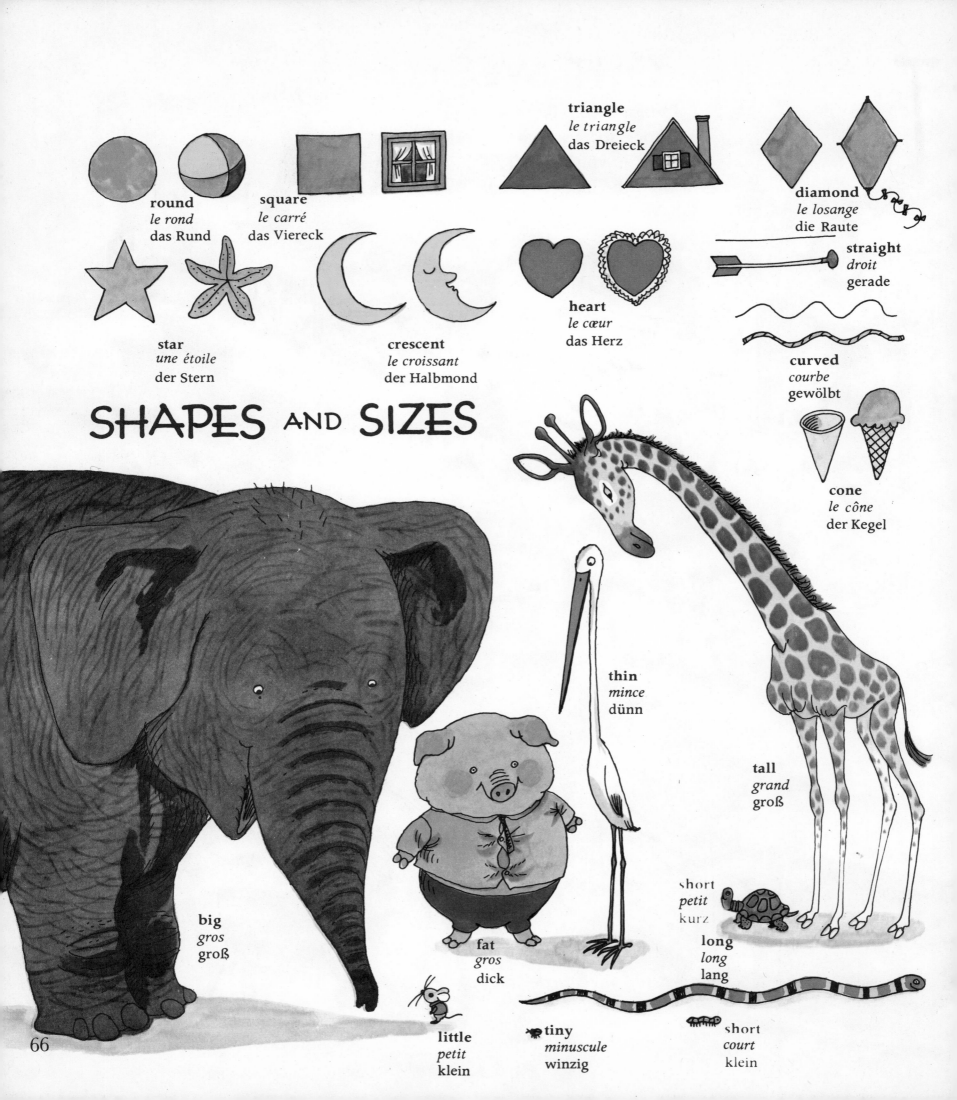

round
le rond
das Rund

square
le carré
das Viereck

triangle
le triangle
das Dreieck

diamond
le losange
die Raute

star
une étoile
der Stern

crescent
le croissant
der Halbmond

heart
le cœur
das Herz

straight
droit
gerade

curved
courbe
gewölbt

cone
le cône
der Kegel

SHAPES AND SIZES

big
gros
groß

thin
mince
dünn

tall
grand
groß

fat
gros
dick

short
petit
kurz

long
long
lang

little
petit
klein

tiny
minuscule
winzig

short
court
klein

THE BABY

father
le père
der Vater

mother
la mère
die Mutter

That cat family has a new baby kitten.
They don't know what to name it.
What would you like
to name the new baby?
Write the kitten's name here.

_____

uncle
l'oncle
der Onkel

grandmother
la grand-mère
die Großmutter

bottle
un biberon
eine Flasche

baby
le bébé
das Baby

rattle
un hochet
eine Rassel

sister
la sœur
die Schwester

brother
le frère
der Bruder

nappy
le lange
die Windel

aunt
la tante
die Tante

grandfather
le grand-père
der Großvater

playpen
le parc à bébé
der Laufstall

cousin
le cousin
der Vetter

high chair
la chaise haute
der Kinderstuhl

cot
le lit d'enfant
das Kinderbett

pushchair
la poussette
der Sportwagen

cradle
le berceau
der Korbwagen

play table
la table à jeu
der Spieltisch

walker
le trotteur
der Laufring

pram
le landau
der Kinderwagen

67

AT THE CIRCUS

The band is playing and the animals are doing their acts. What do you like to watch best at the circus?

balancing pole
le balancier
die Balancierstange

tightrope performer
le funambule
der Seilakrobat

tent pole
le mât de tente
die Zeltstange

tightrope
la corde
das Seil

band
l'orchestre
die Kapelle

acrobat
une acrobate
eine Akrobatin

rope ladder
une échelle de corde
eine Strickleiter

bandstand
une estrade
das Podium

circus horse
le cheval de cirque
das Zirkuspferd

performing elephant
un éléphant savant
ein dressierter Elefant

ring
la piste
die Manege

sawdust
la sciure de bois
das Sägemehl

ringmaster
le directeur de piste
der Zirkusdirektor

performing dog
le chien savant
der Zirkushund

clown

clown
le clown
der Clown

pennant
le fanion
der Wimpel

circus tent
le chapiteau
das Zirkuszelt

trapeze
le trapèze
das Trapez

trapeze artist
le trapéziste
der Trapezkünstler

acrobat
une acrobate
eine Akrobatin

safety net
le filet
das Netz

ticket seller
le caissier
der Kartenverkäufer

hoop
un cerceau
der Ring

lion
le lion
der Löwe

whip
le fouet
die Peitsche

cage
la cage
der Käfig

juggler
le jongleur
der Jongleur

lion tamer
le dompteur
der Löwenbändiger

trained sealion
une otarie savante
ein dressierter Seelöwe

balloon man
un marchand
de ballons
ein Luftballon-
verkäufer

sweets
des bonbons
die Süßwaren

69

SPORTS

bat
la batte
das Schlagholz

ball
la balle
der Ball

wicket keeper
le garde-guichet
der Torwart

cricket
le cricket
das Kricket

batsman
le batteur
der Schläger

wicket
le guichet
der Dreistab

sports ground
le terrain de jeux
der Sportplatz

goalkeeper
le gardien de but
der Torwart

referee
un arbitre
der Schiedsrichter

football
le football
der Fußball

goal
le but
das Tor

whistle
le sifflet
die Pfeife

striker
un avant
der Stürmer

70

racket
la raquette
der Schläger

net
le filet
das Netz

tennis
le tennis
das Tennis

cabbage
le chou
der Kohl

basketball
le basket
das Korbballspiel

hockey
le hockey
das Hockeyspiel

table tennis
le ping-pong
das Tischtennis

handlebars
le guidon
die Lenkstange

bicycle
la bicyclette
das Fahrrad

cycling
le cyclisme
das Radfahren

71

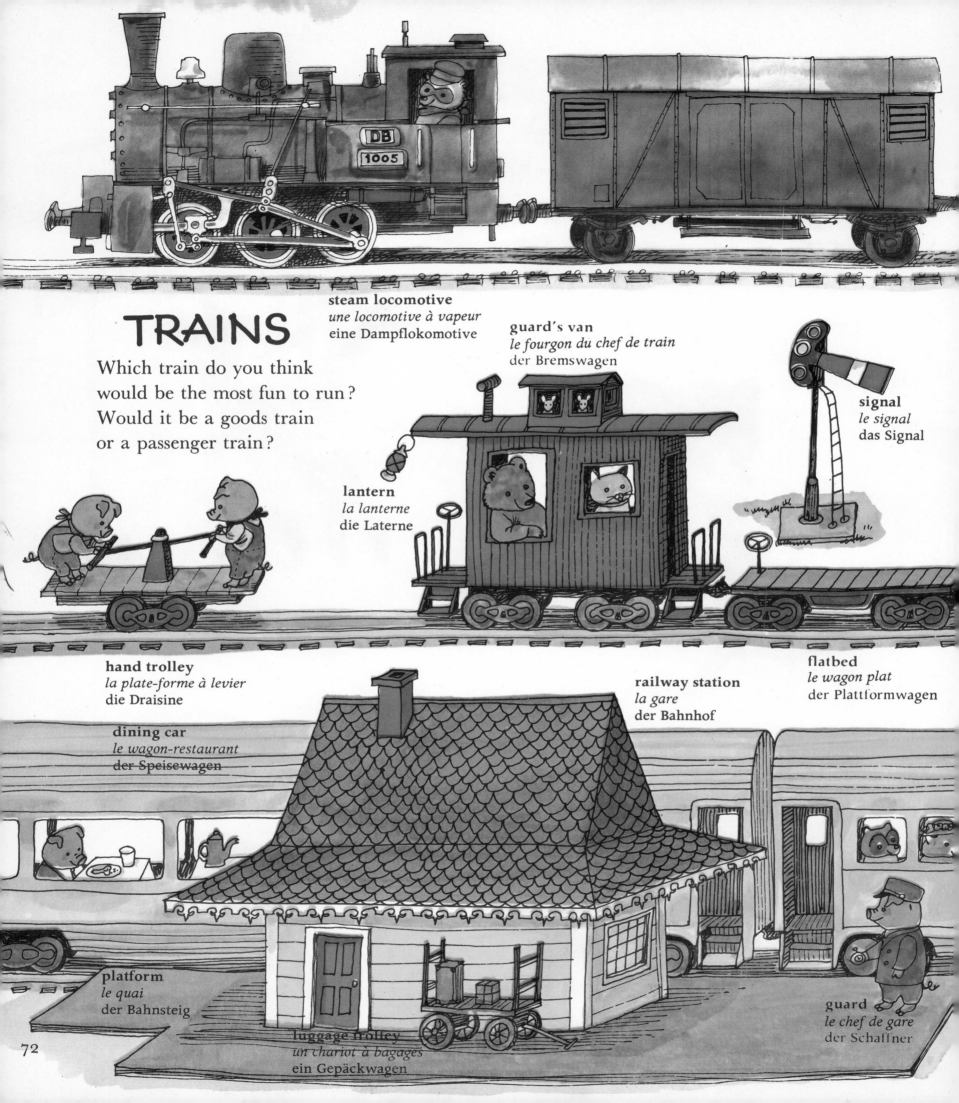

TRAINS

steam locomotive
une locomotive à vapeur
eine Dampflokomotive

Which train do you think
would be the most fun to run?
Would it be a goods train
or a passenger train?

guard's van
le fourgon du chef de train
der Bremswagen

signal
le signal
das Signal

lantern
la lanterne
die Laterne

hand trolley
la plate-forme à levier
die Draisine

railway station
la gare
der Bahnhof

flatbed
le wagon plat
der Plattformwagen

dining car
le wagon-restaurant
der Speisewagen

platform
le quai
der Bahnsteig

luggage trolley
un chariot à bagages
ein Gepäckwagen

guard
le chef de gare
der Schaffner

72

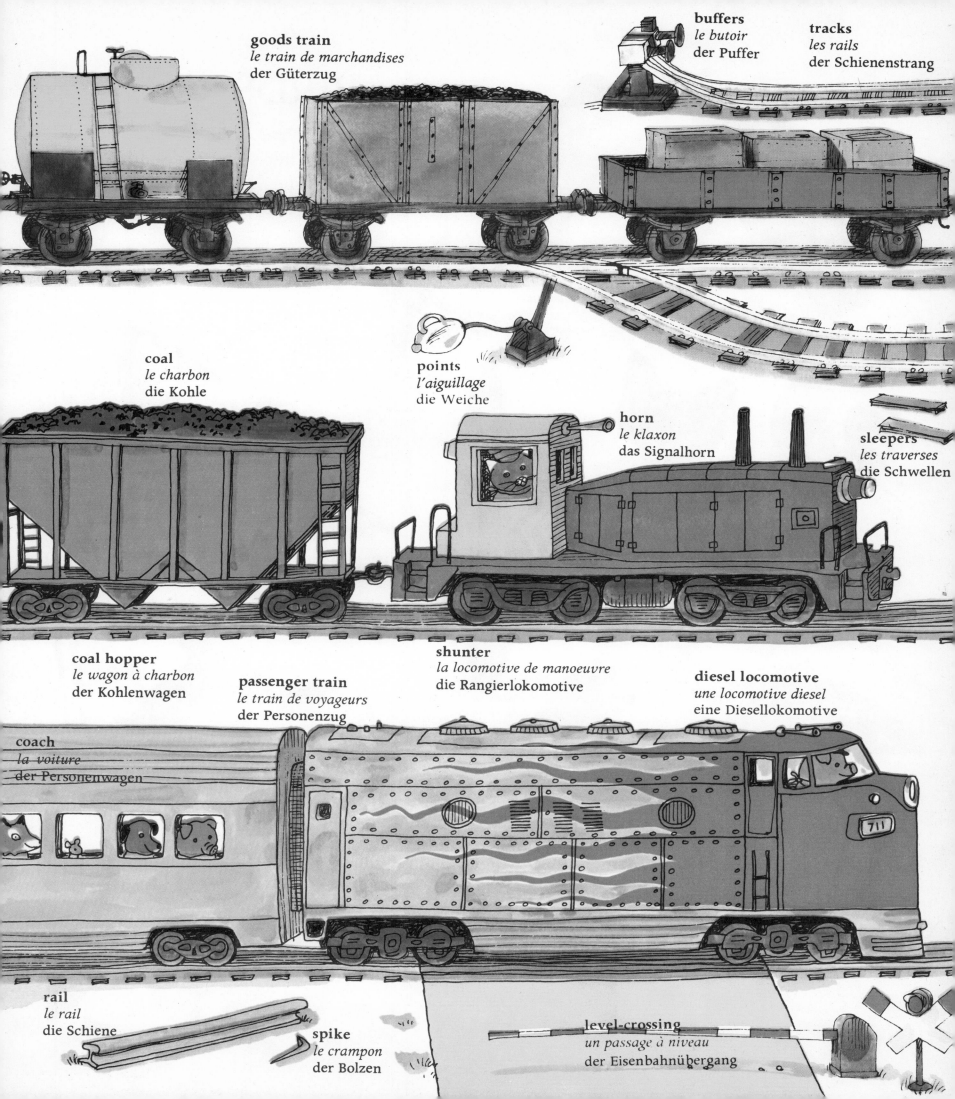

goods train
le train de marchandises
der Güterzug

buffers
le butoir
der Puffer

tracks
les rails
der Schienenstrang

coal
le charbon
die Kohle

points
l'aiguillage
die Weiche

horn
le klaxon
das Signalhorn

sleepers
les traverses
die Schwellen

coal hopper
le wagon à charbon
der Kohlenwagen

passenger train
le train de voyageurs
der Personenzug

shunter
la locomotive de manoeuvre
die Rangierlokomotive

diesel locomotive
une locomotive diesel
eine Diesellokomotive

coach
la voiture
der Personenwagen

rail
le rail
die Schiene

spike
le crampon
der Bolzen

level-crossing
un passage à niveau
der Eisenbahnübergang

BIRDS

Most birds can fly. Some birds can't fly.
One bird who can't fly lives at the South Pole.
He likes to slide on the ice. Which bird is it?

eagle
un aigle
der Adler

hawk
le faucon
der Falke

hummingbird
un oiseau-mouche
der Kolibri

swallow
une hirondelle
eine Schwalbe

heron
le héron
der Reiher

cock
le coq
der Hahn

nuthatch
le pic bleu
der Kleiber

hen
la poule
die Henne

chick
le poussin
das Küken

goose
une oie
der Gans

pigeon
le pigeon
die Taube

duck
le canard
die Ente

woodpeckers
des piverts
die Spechte

flamingo
le flamant
der Flamingo

spoonbill
la spatule
der Löffelreiher

swan
le cygne
der Schwan

duckling
le caneton
das Entenküken

bittern
le butor
die Rohrdommel

penguin
le pingouin
der Pinguin

pelican
le pélican
der Pelikan

vulture
le vautour
der Geier

parrot
le perroquet
der Papagei

crow
la corneille
die Krähe

owl
le hibou
die Eule

toucan
le toucan
der Tukan

dove
la colombe
die Taube

puffin
le puffin
der Papageitaucher

bullfinch
le bouvreuil
der Gimpel

cardinal
le cardinal
der Kardinal

jay
le geai
der Häher

robin
le rouge-gorge
das Rotkehlchen

sparrow
le moineau
der Spatz

wren
le roitelet
der Zaunkönig

tern
une hirondelle de mer
eine Seeschwalbe

sandpiper
le bécasseau
der Strandläufer

sea gull
une mouette
eine Möwe

canary
le canari
der Kanarienvogel

bird house
la volière
das Vogelhäuschen

bird cage
la cage
der Vogelkäfig

nest
le nid
das Nest

baby birds
des oisillons
die Vogeljungen

quail
la caille
die Wachtel

pheasant
le faisan
der Fasan

egret
une aigrette
der Silberreiher

stork
la cigogne
der Storch

ostrich
une autruche
der Strauß

woodcock
la bécasse
die Waldschnepfe

ostrich egg
un oeuf d'autruche
das Straußenei

75

AT THE BEACH

In the summertime it is fun
to go to the beach.
What do you think
Rabbit hears in the seashell?
Is it the sound of the waves?

telescope
la longue-vue
das Fernrohr

lighthouse
le phare
des Leuchtturm

summer cottage
une maisonnette
das Sommerhäuschen

oar
la rame
das Ruder

anchor
une ancre
der Anker

rubber ring
*une bouée en
caoutchouc*
ein Gummitier

spade
une pelle
eine Schaufel

rowing boat
la barque
das Ruderboot

sandpiper
le bécasseau
der Strandläufer

sand castle
un château de sable
eine Sandburg

waves
des vagues
die Wellen

skate
la raie
der Rochen

mackerel
le maquereau
die Makrele

oyster
une huître
eine Auster

lobster
le homard
der Hummer

scallop
la coquille Saint-Jacques
die Kammuschel

clam
la palourde
die Venusmuschel

sea purse
un oreiller de mer
das Haifischei

hermit crab
le bernard-l'ermite
der Einsiedlerkrebs

umbrella
le parasol
der Sonnenschirm

sea gull
la mouette
die Möwe

sun
le soleil
die Sonne

shelter
la cabane
der Pavillon

flag pole
le mât
der Fahnenmast

lifeguard
un maître nageur
ein Badewärter

promenade
le chemin de planches
die Strandpromenade

sand dune
une dune
die Düne

beach grass
les ajoncs
der Strandhafer

stairs
un escalier
eine Treppe

beach chair
le siège pliant
der Liegestuhl

bathing house
les cabines de bain
die Badekabinen

sea shell
la conque marine
die Muschel

starfish
une étoile de mer
der Seestern

sand dugout
une excavation
eine Sandburg

waves
des vagues
die Wellen

prawn
une crevette
eine Krabbe

sprat
le harenguet
die Sprotte

horseshoe crab
le limule
der Schwertschwanz

crab
le crabe
der Krebs

seaweed
les algues
der Tang

mussel
la moule
die Miesmuschel

flounder
le flet
die Flunder

77

HOUSES

In different parts of the world
people live in different kinds of houses.
If you were invited to visit one of these houses,
which would you like to stay in?

igloo
un igloo
eine Schneehütte

tree house
la cabane indienne
das Baumhaus

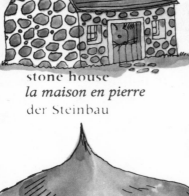

stone house
la maison en pierre
der Steinbau

mud hut
une hutte en boue séchée
eine Lehmhütte

stilt house
la hutte sur pilotis
der Pfahlbau

desert tent
la tente saharienne
das Wüstenzelt

grass house
la paillote
die Grashütte

wooden frame house
la maison en bois
das Holzhaus

Mongolian tent
une yourte mongole
ein mongolisches Zelt

castle
le château fort
das Schloß

half-timbered house
la maison à colombage
das Fachwerkhaus

Mexican adobe house
la maison d'adobe mexicane
mexikanischer Lehmbau

thatched-roof cottage
la chaumière
das Strohdachhaus

chalet
le chalet
das Schweizerhaus

brick house
la maison de brique
der Backsteinbau

"sampan" houseboat
un sampan chinois
ein chinesisches Wohnboot

block of flats
un immeuble moderne
der Wohnblock

modern house
la villa moderne
das moderne Haus

MAKING THINGS GROW

water main
la conduite d'eau
die Wasserleitung

nozzle
*une lance
d'arrosage*
eine Düse

Everyone is working in the garden.
Mr Crow has a seed in his mouth.
Do you think he will plant it?
Or will he eat it?

maize
du maïs
der Mais

hose
le tuyau
der Gartenschlauch

gardener
le jardinier
der Gärtner

spade
la bêche
der Spaten

string
une corde
eine Schnur

hoe
une binette
eine Hacke

tomato plants
les plants de tomate
die Tomatenpflanzen

seed row
le sillon
die Furche

seeds
les graines
die Samen

seedlings
les jeunes plants
die Sämlinge

handle
la poignée
der Griff

rake
le râteau
der Rechen

stake
le piquet
der Holzpflock

stones
les cailloux
die Steine

garden fork
la fourche
die Forke

BEETS

TOMATOES

fertilizer trolley
le chariot à engrais
der Kunstdünger-Karren

80

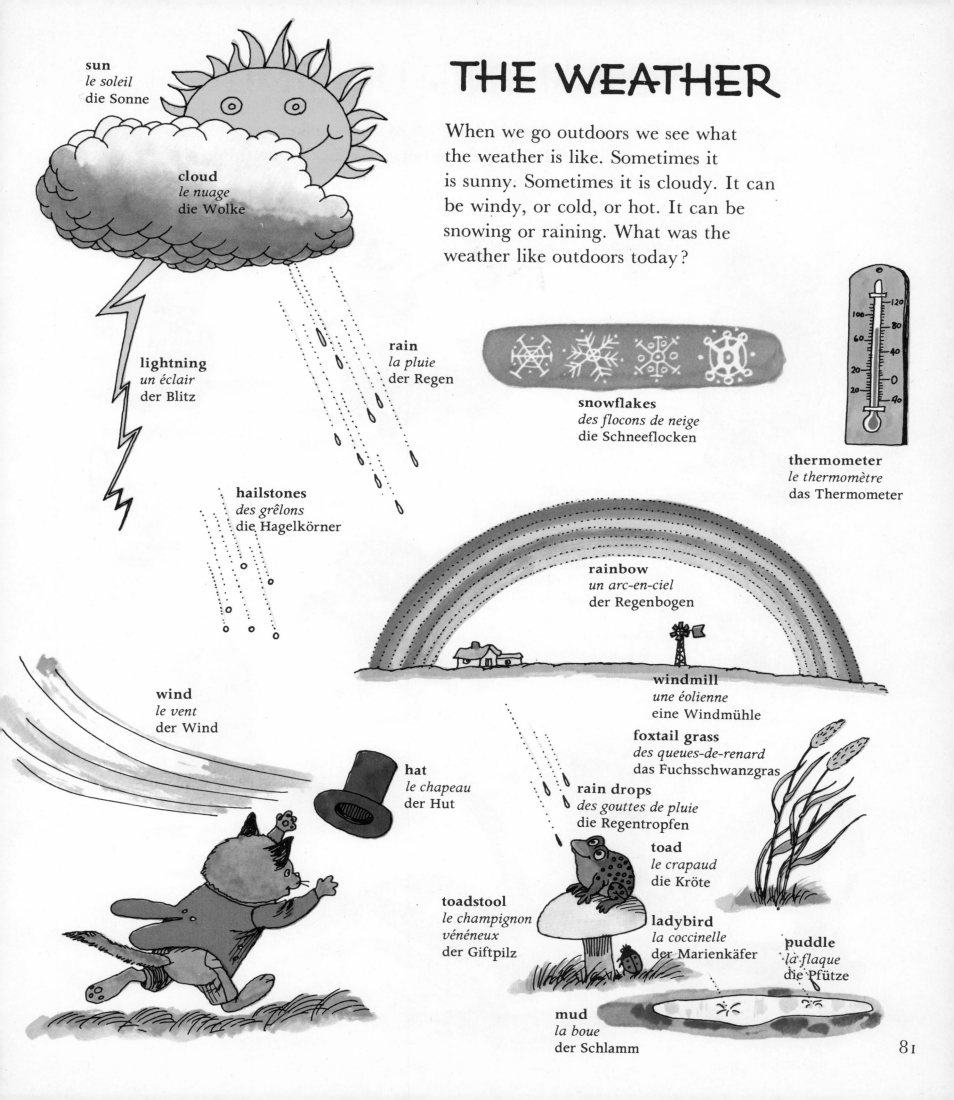

THE WEATHER

When we go outdoors we see what the weather is like. Sometimes it is sunny. Sometimes it is cloudy. It can be windy, or cold, or hot. It can be snowing or raining. What was the weather like outdoors today?

sun
le soleil
die Sonne

cloud
le nuage
die Wolke

lightning
un éclair
der Blitz

rain
la pluie
der Regen

hailstones
des grêlons
die Hagelkörner

snowflakes
des flocons de neige
die Schneeflocken

thermometer
le thermomètre
das Thermometer

rainbow
un arc-en-ciel
der Regenbogen

windmill
une éolienne
eine Windmühle

wind
le vent
der Wind

hat
le chapeau
der Hut

foxtail grass
des queues-de-renard
das Fuchsschwanzgras

rain drops
des gouttes de pluie
die Regentropfen

toad
le crapaud
die Kröte

toadstool
le champignon vénéneux
der Giftpilz

ladybird
la coccinelle
der Marienkäfer

puddle
la flaque
die Pfütze

mud
la boue
der Schlamm

81

CLEANING-UP TIME

Each of the animals has a job to do to make everything tidy around the house. What do you think each animal is about to do?

mop
le balai à franges
der Mop

cleaning powder
la poudre a récurer
das Putzpulver

glue
la colle
der Leim

sponge
une éponge
der Schwamm

spilt water
de l'eau renversée
vergossenes Wasser

adjustable spanner
la clef à molette
der Engländer

coat hanger
le cintre
der Kleiderbügel

waste paper
de vieux papiers
das Abfallpapier

glasses
les lunettes
die Brille

hammer
le marteau
der Hammer

torn sheet
un drap déchiré
ein zerrissenes Laken

sewing machine
la machine à coudre
die Nähmaschine

chipped vase
un vase ébréché
eine angeschlagene Vase

These boots are muddy.
Ces bottines sont couvertes de boue.
Diese Stiefel sind schmutzig.

paw prints
des traces de pattes
die Pfotenabdrücke

footprints
des traces de pas
die Fußstapfen

clothes rail
la tringle
die Kleiderstange

The table leg is broken.
La table a perdu un pied.
Das Tischbein ist abgebrochen

leaking tap
un robinet qui goutte
ein tropfender Wasserhahn

brush
la brosse
die Bürste

dustpan
le ramasse-poussière
die Kehrschaufel

waste paper basket
la corbeille à papier
der Papierkorb

ashes
les cendres
die Asche

book
le livre
das Buch

bookcase
la bibliothèque
der Bücherschrank

old newspapers
de vieux journaux
alte Zeitungen

old magazines
de vieilles revues
alte Zeitscriften

lots of coat hangers
beaucoup de cintres
viele Kleiderbügel

dustbin
la poubelle
die Mülltonne

83

kite
le cerf-volant
der Drachen

rain shower
une averse
der Regenschauer

buds
les bourgeons
die Knospen

robin
le rouge-gorge
das Rotkehlchen

SPRING

Look at that baby lamb hop!
It is spring. He is happy.
Look at Mr Bear coming out of
his cave! It is spring.
Now he can use his new
lawn mower.

lamb
un agneau
das Lamm

bush
un arbuste
der Busch

brook
le ruisseau
der Bach

bridge
un pont
eine Brücke

fern
des fougères
der Farn

roots
des racines
die Wurzeln

tortoise
la tortue
die Schildkröte

cave
une caverne
eine Höhle

frog
la grenouille
der Frosch

daffodils
les jonquilles
die Osterglocken

pussy willow
les chatons de saule
die Weidenkätzchen

lawn mower
la tondeuse à gazon
der Rasenmäher

crocus
le crocus
der Krokus

violets
les violettes
die Veilchen

84

SUMMER

Do you like to go
on picnics in the summer time?
Ants just love to go to picnics.
Do you know why?

cow
la vache
die Kuh

cornfield
le champ de blé
.das Maisfeld

meadow
le pré
die Wiese

calf
le veau
der Kalb

fence
la clôture
der Zaun

station wagon
le break
der Kombiwagen

tent
la tente
das Zelt

camp bed
le lit de camp
das Feldbett

fly
une mouche
eine Fliege

grill
le gril
das Grill

picnic basket
le panier de pique-nique
der Picknickkorb

charcoal
le charbon de bois
die Holzkohle

water carrier
le tonnelet d'eau
der Wasserbehälter

ham roll
un sandwich au jambon
eine Schinkensemmel

sausages
des saucisses
die Würstchen

pickle
le cornichon
die saure Gurke

mustard
la moutarde
der Senf

ketchup
le ketchup
das Tomatenketchup

paper cup
le gobelet en carton
der Papierbecher

mosquito
le moustique
die Stechmücke

fishing rod
la canne à pêche
die Angel

rock
le rocher
der Felsen

ants
les fourmis
die Ameisen

bulrushes
les joncs
das Schilf

float
le flotteur
der Schwimmer

pond
un étang
der Teich

frog
la grenouille
der Frosch

landing stage
le ponton
der Anlegeplatz

water lily
le nénuphar
die Wasserrose

dragonfly
la libellule
die Libelle

pebbles
des cailloux
die Kieselsteine

stones
les pierres
die Steine

85

sun
le soleil
die Sonne

pheasant
le faisan
der Fasan

falling leaves
des feuilles mortes
fallende Blätter

stone wall
le mur
die Steinmauer

grouse
le tétras
das Moorhuh

nuts
des noix
die Nüsse

gate
la barrière
das Tor

corn on the cob
des épis de maïs
die Maiskolben

AUTUMN

In the autumn the air gets
colder. The green leaves turn to
bright colours. Then they fall to
the ground. Who is raking
them all up?

cider
le cidre
der Apfelsaft

jam
la confiture
die Marmelade

smoke
la fumée
der Rauch

flames
des flammes
die Flammen

basket of apples
un panier de pommes
ein Korb mit Äpfeln

turkey
le dindon
der Truthahn

rake
le râteau
der Rechen

bonfire
le feu
das Herbstfeuer

86
leaves
les feuilles
die Blätter

snowstorm
la tempête de neige
der Schneesturm

WINTER

There are many ways to
have fun on the snow and ice.
Maybe you would like to do
all of them. Would you?

sleigh
le traîneau
der Schlitten

icicle
le glaçon
der Eiszapfen

sledge
la luge
der Rodelschlitten

fishing hut
la cabane de pêche
die Fischerhütte

skis
des skis
die Skier

toboggan
le toboggan
der Toboggan

ice fishing
pêcher sous la glace
unterm Eis fischen

ice-skating rink
la piste de patinage
die Eisbahn

snow ball
la boule de neige
der Schneeball

hockey stick
la crosse de hockey
der Hockeyschläger

nuffler
ne écharpe
n laine
ler Wollschal

puck
le palet
das Puck

spare tyre
la roue
de secours
das Reserverad

ice skates
les patins à glace
die Schlittschuhe

jeep
la jeep
der Jeep

snowplough
le chasse-neige
der Schneepflug

a pig all wrapped up
un cochon tout emmitouflé
ein eingemummtes Schwen

snowman
le bonhomme de neige
der Schneemann

87

LITTLE THINGS

Here are many little things.
What little thing do you sometimes
put on your Mummy's wall?

reel
la bobine
der Haspel

button
le bouton
der Knopf

dandelion seed
la graine de pissenlit
der Löwenzahnsamen

worm
le ver de terre
der Wurm

thread
le fil
der Faden

fly
la mouche
die Fliege

ant
la fourmi
die Ameise

drop of water
la goutte d'eau
das Tröpfchen

ladybird
la coccinelle
die Marienkäfer

bead
la perle
die Perle

snowflake
le cristal de neige
die Schneeflocke

pin
une épingle
eine Stecknadel

fingerprint
une empreinte digitale
der Fingerabdruck

petal
le pétale
das Blumenblatt

mosquito
le moustique
der Moskito

butterfly
le papillon
der Schmetterling

fish-hook
un hameçon
der Angelhaken

crumb
la miette
die Krume

soap bubble
une bulle de savon
die Seifenblase

peanut
la cacahouète
die Erdnuß

tack
la punaise
der Stift

pen nib
la plume de stylo
die Federspitze

tea leaf
la feuille de thé
das Teeblatt

gumdrop
la boule de gomme
der Gummibonbon

pea
le petit pois
die Erbse

caterpillar
la chenille
die Raupe

pill
la pilule
die Pille

firefly
la luciole
der Leuchtkäfer

ring
la bague
der Ring

sand
le sable
der Sand

sloe
la prunelle
die Schlehe

moth
la phalène
die Motte

rice
des grains de riz
der Reis

tadpole
le têtard
die Kaulquappe

keyhole
le trou de serrure
das Schlüsselloch

shell
la coquille
die Muschel

marble
la bille
die Murmel

blade of grass
le brin d'herbe
der Grashalm

paper clip
le trombone
die Büroklammer

cricket
le criquet
die Grille

raisin
le raisin sec
die Rosine

beetle
le scarabée
der Käfer

raspberry
la framboise
die Himbeere

thimble
le dé
der Fingerhut

pincushion
la pelote à épingles
das Nadelkissen

hermit crab
le bernard-l'hermite
der Einsiedlerkrebs

pebble
le caillou
der Kieselstein

sea horse
un hippocampe
das Seepferdchen

bee
une abeille
die Biene

mushroom
le champignon
der Pilz

pearl
la perle fine
die Perle

ink spot
la tâche d'encre
der Tintenfleck

confetti
les confetti
das Konfetti

feather
la plume d'oiseau
die Feder

splinter
une écharde
der Splitter

bean
le haricot
die Bohne

safety pin
une épingle anglaise
die Sicherheitsnadel

baby mouse
le souriceau
das Mäuschen

dot
le point
der Punkt

88

PARTS OF THE BODY

Bear picks things up in his paws.
What do you pick things up with?

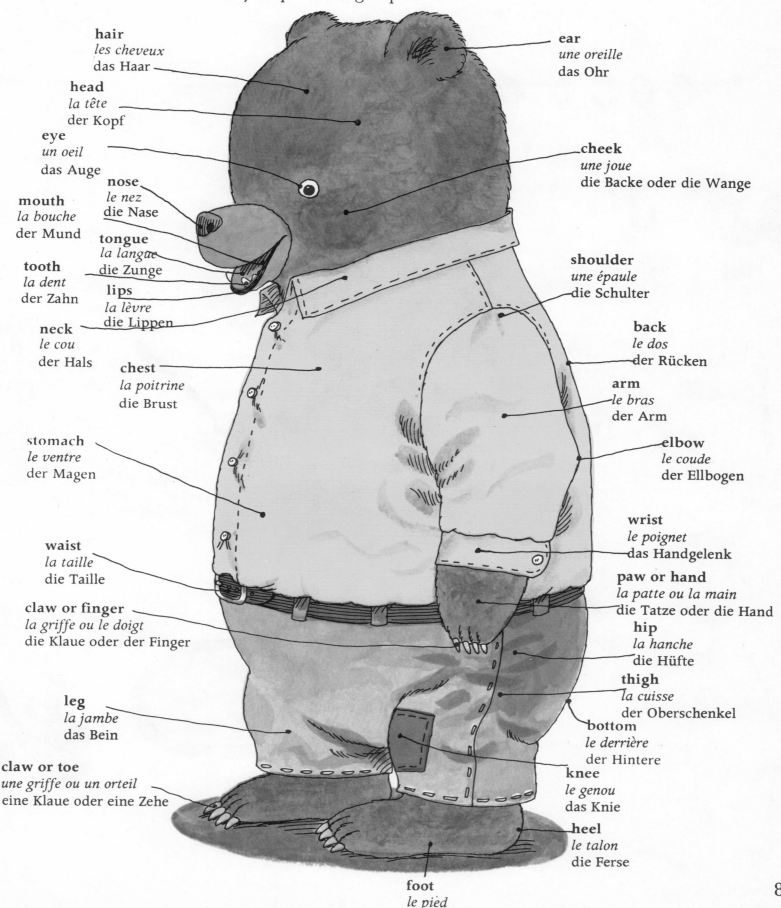

hair
les cheveux
das Haar

head
la tête
der Kopf

eye
un oeil
das Auge

nose
le nez
die Nase

mouth
la bouche
der Mund

tongue
la langue
die Zunge

tooth
la dent
der Zahn

lips
la lèvre
die Lippen

neck
le cou
der Hals

chest
la poitrine
die Brust

stomach
le ventre
der Magen

waist
la taille
die Taille

claw or finger
la griffe ou le doigt
die Klaue oder der Finger

leg
la jambe
das Bein

claw or toe
une griffe ou un orteil
eine Klaue oder eine Zehe

ear
une oreille
das Ohr

cheek
une joue
die Backe oder die Wange

shoulder
une épaule
die Schulter

back
le dos
der Rücken

arm
le bras
der Arm

elbow
le coude
der Ellbogen

wrist
le poignet
das Handgelenk

paw or hand
la patte ou la main
die Tatze oder die Hand

hip
la hanche
die Hüfte

thigh
la cuisse
der Oberschenkel

bottom
le derrière
der Hintere

knee
le genou
das Knie

heel
le talon
die Ferse

foot
le pied
der Fuß

89

BEDTIME

Who is that hiding under the bed?
Find the naughty rascal and tell him to brush his
teeth and get into bed.

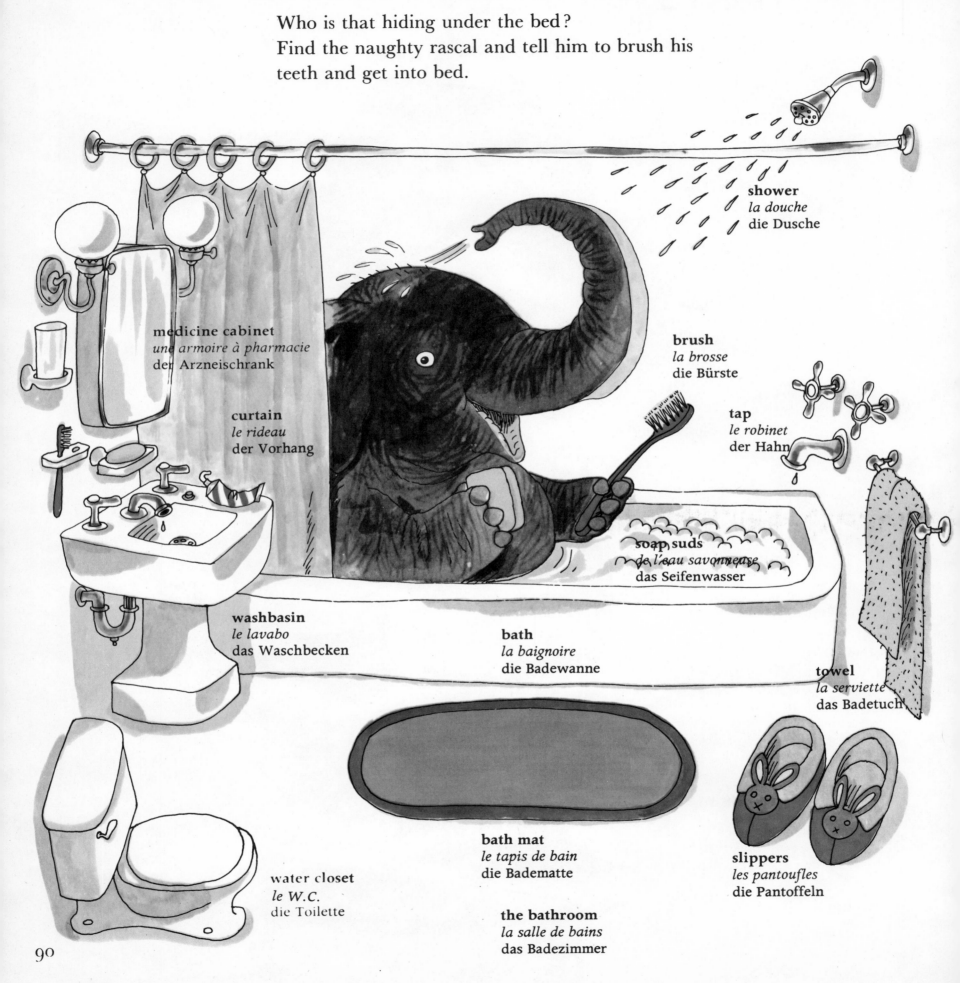

shower
la douche
die Dusche

medicine cabinet
une armoire à pharmacie
der Arzneischrank

brush
la brosse
die Bürste

curtain
le rideau
der Vorhang

tap
le robinet
der Hahn

soap suds
de l'eau savonneuse
das Seifenwasser

washbasin
le lavabo
das Waschbecken

bath
la baignoire
die Badewanne

towel
la serviette
das Badetuch

water closet
le W.C.
die Toilette

bath mat
le tapis de bain
die Badematte

slippers
les pantoufles
die Pantoffeln

the bathroom
la salle de bains
das Badezimmer

ceiling
le plafond
die Decke

wall
le mur
die Wand

Mummy
maman
Mutti

moon
la lune
der Mond

stars
les étoiles
die Sterne

painting
le tableau
das Gemälde

book
le livre
das Buch

pillow
un oreiller
das Kopfkissen

366
GOODNIGHT
STORIES

toy
la poupée
das Spielzeug

blanket
la couverture
die Bettdecke

sheet
le drap
das Bettuch

mousehole
le trou de souris
das Mauseloch

chest of drawers
la commode
die Kommode

bed
le lit
das Bett

rug
la descente de lit
die Brücke

91

THE LAST WORDS OF THE DAY

the chick
le poussin
das Küken

the piglet
le cochonnet
das Schweinchen

the dog
le chien
der Hund

the cat
le chat (la chatte)
die Katze

the hen
la poule
die Henne

the bear
l'ours
der Bär

the bee
l'abeille
die Biene

the rabbit
le lapin
der Hase

the fox
le renard
der Fuchs

the duck
le canard
die Ente

the mouse
la souris
die Maus

the owl
le hibou
die Eule

the frog
la grenouille
der Frosch

all say   **GOODNIGHT!**
disent tous   **BONNE NUIT!**
sagen alle   **GUTE NACHT!**

Walrus has some last words, too.
Le morse a aussi quelque chose
à dire avant de nous quitter.
Das Walroß hat noch etwas wichtiges
zum Abschluß zu sagen.

Do you know what he is saying?
Savez-vous ce que c'est?
Weißt Du, was es ist?

cock
le coq
der Hahn

hen
la poule
die Henne

chick
le poussin
das Küken

mole
la taupe
der Maulwurf

letter
la lettre
der Brief

guitarist
le guitariste
der Gitarrenspieler

crow
une corneille
eine Krähe

rabbit
le lapin
der Hase

spade
la bêche
der Spaten

fly
une mouche
eine Fliege

umbrella
le parapluie
der Schirm

vase
un vase
eine Vase

pig
le cochon
das Schwein

mouse
la souris
die Maus

lamb
un agneau
das Lamm

walrus
le morse
das Walroß